The International Brotherhood of Teamsters

ONE OF A SERIES OF STUDIES OF COMPARATIVE UNION
GOVERNMENTS EDITED BY WALTER GALENSON FOR THE
CENTER FOR THE STUDY OF DEMOCRATIC INSTITUTIONS

The International
Brotherhood of
Teamsters:

Its Government and Structure

Sam Romer

196150

John Wiley and Sons, Inc.

New York and London

Library of Congress Catalog Card Number: 62–20168
Printed in the United States of America

Foreword

The nation's press has probably written more about the Teamsters Union under Dave Beck and James R. Hoffa than about any other American trade union in our history. Not even John L. Lewis, in the days when he was regularly defying the President of the United States, made the headlines as regularly. The press accounts have been almost solidly negative; they have emphasized charges of corruption and alleged ties with the underworld, the threat to the American economy posed by the union's bargaining power, the lack of democratic procedure within the organization. The public image of the Teamsters Union could hardly be worse.

Despite the barrage of anti-Teamster publicity, the union has been doing quite well. It is one of the few American unions to have maintained a forward momentum during the last decade. In addition to truck drivers, employees in an amazing variety of industries have been attracted by its success as a collective bargainer. Perhaps it is a case of the advantages of publicity, good or bad; but the fact that Hoffa sharply increased the union's expenditures for organizational work undoubtedly contributed to the rise in the trend of membership.

One quickly discovers, in reading through what has been written about the Teamsters, that it is difficult to secure any information about how the organization operates, despite the fact that it is one of the largest private associations in the country. What is its constitution like? Is it more or less democratic than those of other trade unions? To what extent is there any internal political life, in terms of contests for office, opposition blocs, turnover of officials? Is the day-to-day business run efficiently? How much money does the union take in, how is it spent and invested? It is to these and similar questions that this monograph is devoted, although Mr. Romer never loses sight of the broader issues.

What emerges is not particularly encouraging for those who are concerned with the future of union democracy; but neither is it all black. The union's convention, because of its size and the composition of its membership (practically all the delegates are full-time officials), provides little challenge to the leadership—but this is generally true throughout the labor movement. As to the conduct of the convention, a delegate to the 1961 gathering remarked: "I don't think I have witnessed a chairman that has allowed more democracy to creep in here"—but at least some did creep in. The general executive board is by no stretch of the imagination an effective counterweight to the president, but neither is it a completely subservient rubber stamp. It includes among its members "idealists and intellectuals" as well as some who "are in great measure tied to underworld characters, men in the uneasy shadows of the sport world, and the 'fixers' of a corrupt business environment." The union pays high salaries and provides liberal expense accounts, but neither the labor movement nor the business community has ever considered this a cardinal sin.

Mr. Romer concludes that the Teamsters Union "is neither the model of a democratic, idealistic unionism which stirs our hearts and hopes, nor is it the impressive juggernaut which crushes beneath its flanged wheels any display of membership initiative or individual non-conformism." Some locals are "festering sores of racketeering and corruption," but others are honestly run and offer their members a broad range of services. The fundamental problem, as Mr. Romer sees it, is not so much the practices which have been high-lighted by the McClellan Committee as the tendency of the members to look upon the union as a kind of auto club. They are interested only in a limited range of services, and as long as these are forthcoming in a reasonably effective fashion, they are not at all concerned with the way the or-ganization is run, any more than the average auto club member knows—or cares—how the policies of the organiza-tion which he helps support are formulated. The Teamsters Union, in its way, is a pioneer of this type of unionism. Both Beck and Hoffa made no bones about the fact that they were in business—the business of selling labor—and if alongside their main wares they were engaged in selling other goods which yielded personal profits, what harm to the mem-bers? It is important to understand that this new unionism has quite a different set of ethical standards from the tradi-tional American business unionism of Samuel Gompers, William Green, and John L. Lewis.

The present book is one of a series of monographs on trade union goverment in the United States, commissioned by the Trade Union Study of the Center for the Study of Democratic Institutions, and supported by a grant from the Fund for the Republic. The views and judgments expressed are those of the author and not necessarily of the Center or the Fund. Sam Romer brings to this work a lifetime of study of the labor movement from his vantage point as labor reporter of the *Minneapolis Tribune*. The Teamsters Union has been a particular interest of his over the years, and he has followed its development closely. This slender book is the most objective and scholarly study that has yet been done of the Teamsters Union, in my estimation, and I am certain that the reader, when he has finished it, will join with me in thanking Mr. Romer for a pleasurable as well as a profitable experience.

WALTER GALENSON

Preface

Much of the material in this book is based on personal observations and experiences. As labor reporter for the *Minneapolis Tribune,* I covered the 1952, 1957, and 1961 conventions of the International Union, and annual meetings of the Central and Western Conferences. I interviewed Dan Tobin only once, in the twilight of his career, but both Dave Beck and James Hoffa have been generous in giving me opportunities for interviews and informal chats. With rare exceptions, other staff officials of the International Union, including Harold Gibbons and Einar Mohn, have been cordial and helpful; I am especially grateful to Jake McCarthy, the union's former director of public relations, and James M. Casey, assistant controller, for their patience and understanding. A special word of thanks is due to Gordon Conklin of St. Paul, the union's seventh vice-president and an old and valued friend.

For written source material, I have relied chiefly upon the *International Teamster,* the union's monthly magazine, and published proceedings of the union's conventions and conference meetings. I have also studied with care the thirty-four volumes of testimony which the Senate select committee amassed in its investigation of the Teamsters Union, as well as testimony which concerned other unions. In addition, I have read most of the spate of periodical literature which the committee investigation touched off; many were exaggerated and overdrawn accounts and of no great value. The best of the lot is a series of articles in the *Saturday Evening Post* by John Bartlow Martin, later reprinted in a paperback under the title "Jimmy Hoffa's Hot."

There have been four first-rate published accounts concerning the Teamsters: Robert D. Leiter, *The Teamsters Union;* Nathan P. Feinsinger, *Collective Bargaining in the Trucking Industry;* John B. Gillingham, *The Teamsters Union on the West Coast;* and Samuel E. Hill, *The Teamsters and Transportation.* I have drawn freely from each of them; all four books, however, emphasize the economic aspects rather than the political structure of the union. For general reading in labor, I have relied upon such books as Jack Barbash, *The Practice of Unionism,* William M. Leiserson, *American Trade Union Democracy,* and Philip Taft's two-volume history of the AFL. In addition, I have read widely among other general accounts, and in all cases where I have borrowed ideas or data I have tried to indicate my debt in appropriate reference notes. If I have lapsed occasionally, it was inadvertent and I extend my apologies.

Needless to say, all the conclusions embodied in this book are my own. The book was not intended to be either an exposé of the union or a defense of it; if it will serve to give the reader some understanding of the union's customs and practices, it will have served its purpose.

Sam Romer

Minneapolis, Minn.
September, 1962

Contents

1

The Union

The International Brotherhood of Teamsters is the nation's largest union. It has some 1,700,000 members gathered in 900-odd locals, serviced by a staff of 3,000 organizers and local union business agents. Its growth has been rooted among the men who drive the trucks on city streets and cross-country highways, but it long ago forgot craft exclusiveness and now stretches its claimed jurisdiction to include "all workers, without limitation." James R. Hoffa, the Teamsters' controversial president, can and does evoke scare headlines by a mere pronouncement of new plans; editorial writers, in a kind of conditioned reflex, greet Hoffa's proposals, whether reasonable or far fetched, with hysterical alarm. When Hoffa proposed in 1958 to form a national conference of transportation unions, Senator John L. McClellan (D., Ark.), chairman of the long-lasting Senate investigation into labor racketeering and corruption, reacted instinctively. "All our lives are too intricately interwoven with this union," the senator thundered, "to sit passively by and allow the Teamsters to create a super power in this country, a power greater than the people and greater than the government." [1]

What Hoffa had proposed was far from the "super power" McClellan saw so fearfully. In fact, the proposal to join with the National Maritime Union and the International Long-shoremen's Association was a relatively mild version of similar intra-industry federations long a part of the American labor movement. Moreover, it had little prospect of immediate success. The powerful railroad brotherhoods derided this concept; so did key maritime unions not included in the original announcement. Yet McClellan's warnings were echoed and embellished by Robert F. Kennedy, the Senate committee counsel soon to become United States Attorney General. Kennedy described the proposed conference as "an unholy alliance that could dominate the United States within three to five years" and envisioned "a subversive force of unequalled power in this country." [2]

The explanation for these unrealistic reactions lies in the fact that the Teamsters Union, and Hoffa himself, had been the principal targets of the Senate committee since early in 1957. Much of the committee's findings might be open later to serious question, but their immediate effects were clear. They resulted in an ultimatum from the AFL-CIO to the Teamsters that the union reject Hoffa as president; when the ultimatum was rejected, the AFL-CIO swiftly expelled its largest affiliate. The widespread publicity given the committee's testimony, and Hoffa's refusal or inability to use his constitutional powers as union president to clean up the mess uncovered by committee investigators, led to general public acceptance of the committee's verdict: "That if Hoffa remains unchecked, the tremendous economic power of the Teamsters will place the underworld in a position to dominate American economic life." [3]

But the Teamsters Union, despite its exile from the AFL-CIO and the general condemnation it suffered, appeared to thrive in adversity. John F. English, the union's secretary-treasurer, listed income of $7,106,839 from per capita dues for 1960—the equivalent of 1,480,000 members. It represented an increase of $302,689 since 1958, the first year of Hoffa's regime—or 63,000 members.[4] The figures did not represent a spectacular gain, but they indicated significant growth during a period when many other unions were reporting membership losses. (The union's membership, as reflected in the payment of per capita dues by local unions to international headquarters, varies considerably from month to month because of seasonal fluctuations, especially in the construction and food-processing industries. English put the actual dues-paying membership of the union in November, 1961, at 1,720,562.)[5]

The increase in membership did not come cheaply, English's statistics revealed. From July 1, 1957, through March 31, 1961, the union incurred an operating deficit of $4,623,-307, despite a record $26,106,674 in dues income. In 1960 alone, the operating deficit reached $1,464,854; during 1961, the gap between normal income and expenses widened to $2,606,136. During the 1957 to 1961 period, the operating losses were made up almost entirely by $4,619,035 in receipts from some $30,000,000 in investments, but it was apparent in English's financial report for 1961 that this balance no longer existed. Despite financial income of $1,166,357, the statement disclosed $1,439,259 greater expense than income.[6] It was apparent that a per capita dues increase, passed at the 1961 convention, was necessary to prevent a mounting deficit from eroding the union's financial reserves.

A comparison of the expense statements prepared for the 1957 and 1961 conventions disclosed that keeping and gaining membership was done with dollars, as well as morale. For the 45-month period under Hoffa, $6,794,545 was spent in organizing campaign expenses, compared to $4,996,330 for the full five years previously. Strike benefit payments also were more generous; $6,912,001 was paid out for the 45-month period, compared with a previous $4,083,269 for five years. In addition to these higher costs, the Teamsters paid dearly to cure their legal troubles. During the 45-month period, $2,086,359 was charged to legal fees and expenses, as well as $665,400 charged directly to the Board of Monitors which supervised the union's affairs. Legal fees and expense during the full five-year period before the 1957 convention amounted to $607,335.[7]

The Teamsters Union is a living, continually changing organization. During Hoffa's first 45 months, 62 new locals were chartered and 65 older units dissolved or amalgamated. The same constant flux occurred in the previous five years, when 131 new charters were issued and 141 older ones dropped.[8] The locals range in size from tiny units with so few members that they went unrepresented at the 1961 convention to giant organizations such as Chicago's Local 705 with 17,706 members. Of the five largest locals, incidentally, three are located in Chicago (the others are Locals 710 and 743), the fourth is Hoffa's home Local 299 in Detroit, and the fifth is Philadelphia's Local 107.[9] The concentration of union membership by states corresponds to the general dispersion of the national population. A special report by English in 1959 disclosed that about half of the union's membership is based in five states: California, 235,438; New York, 184,071; Illinois, 152,334; Pennsylvania, 110,434, and Ohio, 84,873.[10] About half of the locals listed in the 1961 delegate list were entitled to but a single delegate, indicating that they had fewer than 1,125 members.[11]

The much-vaunted power of the Teamsters is linked less to its vast membership than to its strategic position in the national economy. "There is simply no substitute for truck transportation," a business magazine noted as early as 1941. "That is the nub of the union's power. Furthermore, it must be supplied continuously. It cannot be stored up like oil or wheat or coal. The railroads may continue to run and carry freight but the Teamsters can effectively halt its movement at any time. In the case of most unions, a strike is just a strike. In the case of the Teamsters, it can be a death warrant for the opposition." [12] This economic power may be exaggerated in many respects, and legal restrictions prohibit-

ing the "hot-cargo" clause and mandating continued com-
mon-carrier operation have blunted its effect. Nevertheless,
Teamsters leaders like to believe it and boast of it. Daniel
J. Tobin, who held the Teamsters' reins for almost a half-
century, was blunt about it. "No other union has the power
that we have," he bragged. "We touch every trade and industry." [13] Einar Mohn, who represented the Teamsters
in the union's futile attempt to avert expulsion from the
AFL-CIO, recalled that "it has become traditional and
customary for labor unions in practically all industries to
call upon the Teamsters local unions for assistance. This is
not stated as a boast but just as a fact of economic life." [14]

There is little evidence that there has been much abuse
of this power. "The Teamsters are not a strike-happy union,"
Hoffa reported to the 1961 convention. Despite the increase
in strike benefit payments, the number of strikes during the
three-year period from 1958 through 1960 averaged only 234
a year and involved a total of 42,000 members, less than 3 per
cent of the union's membership. "Our officers and business
agents," Hoffa asserted, "are realistic and responsible. They
know the industries and companies with whom they deal,
they are familiar with competitive conditions, they are in
touch daily with their membership and understand their
needs." [15]

The beginnings of the Teamsters Union organization in
the United States has been traced to 1850 when San Francisco draymen organized to regulate their charges; a similar
desire to stabilize hack fares led to formation of a local
union of hack owners and drivers in Chicago in 1867. The
union itself urges 1888 as the year of its birth, but the actual
formation of an international union did not come until 1899
when nine locals responded to a call by Samuel Gompers,
president of the American Federation of Labor, and formed
the Team Drivers International Union. The union's membership grew from 1,700 at the founding convention to
13,800 in 1902, but an argument over whether to ban multi-
team owners from membership split the fledgling union.

In 1903, Gompers again intervened and the divided groups re-formed to organize the International Brotherhood of Teamsters.[16]

The union's first few years were not auspicious. "The officers of the International," Tobin—who soon was to take over the union command—later recalled, "seemed to have no other object in view except to enjoy themselves, have a good time, and stopped at nothing to bring about that condition." [17] Cornelius P. Shea of Boston, the union's president, looked the other way while Albert T. Young of Chicago engaged in a dubious alliance with the notorious John G. Driscoll, who headed five separate employer associations. A disastrous strike in Chicago brought in its wake a new secession, and when Tobin defeated Shea for president in 1907 he headed a union more in name than in fact. "We had about 27,000 members," Tobin said later, "and very little in our treasury, and the membership was divided into factions impossible for me to describe or make you understand." [18] But within a year, Tobin had wiped out a $1,000 debt and put $20,000 in the treasury. More important, he conducted a successful campaign against the rebel United Teamsters of America, suffering a brutal personal beating in its course but establishing the Teamsters as a permanent organization.[19]

The advance of the union brought with it a heightened pride. Its 1901 statement of union objectives proposed "to rescue our craft from the low level to which it has fallen" and pledged the organization "to elevate the moral, intellectual, and social conditions of our members." [20] Such self-derogation was eliminated by the 1908 convention which set new goals. These read in part:

"To organize under one banner all workmen engaged in the craft and to educate them to co-operate in every movement which tends to benefit the organization;

"To impress upon the teamsters and the public that a profitable teamster must be honest, sober, intelligent, and naturally adapted to the business;

"To teach them to take advantage of their industrial position and to build up and perfect an impregnable labor organization." [21]

Except for refinement of language, these goals constituted the formal credo of the organization until 1961 when, under Hoffa's leadership, an extensive revision was made. The proud reference to craft was altered to "industry" and the union's objectives were set in so broad a frame as to exclude little from its chartered obligations. "The objects of this International Union," the revised section read, "are also:

"To secure improved wages, hours, working conditions, and other economic advantages through organization, negotiations, and collective bargaining, through advancement of our standing in the community and in the labor movement through legal and economic means, and all other lawful methods;

"To provide educational advancement and training for employes, members, and officers;

"To safeguard, advance, and promote the principle of free collective bargaining, the rights of workers, farmers, and consumers, and the security and welfare of all the people by political, educational, and other community activity;

"To engage in cultural, civic, legislative, political, fraternal, educational, charitable, welfare, social, and other activities which further the interests of this organization and its membership, directly or indirectly;

"To provide financial and moral assistance to other labor organizations or other bodies having purposes or objectives in whole or in part similar or related to those of this organization;

"To engage in community activities which will advance the interests of this organization and its members in the community and the nation, directly or indirectly;

"To protect and preserve the International Union as an institution, and to perform its legal and contractual obligations;

"To receive, manage, invest, expend, or otherwise use the funds and property of this organization to carry out the duties and to achieve the objectives set forth in this International Constitution and By-Laws and for such additional purposes and objects not inconsistent therewith as will further the interests of this organization and its members, directly or indirectly.

"It is recognized that the problems with which this labor organization is accustomed to deal are not limited to unionism or to organization and collective bargaining alone, but encompass a broad spectrum of economic and social objectives as set forth above and as the union may determine from time to time." [22]

The statement of objectives is more than a grandiloquent expression of the union's broad idealism. As with much of the 1961 Constitution, it was a lawyer's document, seeking to prepare a possible defense against later claims that the union leaders had overreached themselves in carrying out their duties. Yet it is clear testimony that unions no longer can limit themselves to a narrow bargaining concept but must adjust to a wide community relationship based on "the security and welfare of all the people."

Until the depression, the Teamsters—except for a short-lived spurt during World War I—failed to make spectacular membership gains. Its total in 1933 was 75,205, barely three times the number Tobin had started with a quarter-century earlier. But it revived quickly during the New Deal unionization drives, doubled its membership by 1935, doubled it again by 1938, and passed the half-million mark by 1941. There was little gain during World War II, but the postwar period saw tremendous organizing gains which carried total membership rolls beyond the million mark by 1950 and to its present peak at 1,700,000 a decade later.[23] The key to this growth lies in the Teamsters' elastic concept of jurisdiction.

The original union constitution disclosed little concern about jurisdiction, as such; its primary emphasis was on requirements for membership eligibility, and it limited its members to "truck, wagon, hack, or vehicle" teamsters, none of whom could own or operate more than five teams. The first mention of jurisdiction came in 1905, when the constitution asserted "jurisdiction over any man driving a team, operating an automobile or any helpers on a wagon or automobile, providing he shall not own or operate more than one team or vehicle." It is worth noting, incidentally, that the new definition of jurisdiction carried with it recognition of the automobile as a factor in the teaming industry. After Tobin assumed international leadership, the jurisdictional claim again was rewritten, this time to a claim "over all teamsters and helpers, chauffeurs and helpers, and men

who are employed on horses, harness, carriages, or automo-
biles, in and around stables or garages." [24]

Despite the principle of exclusive jurisdiction which the
AFL charters supposedly granted, there was little illusion
then (as now) that jurisdictional boundaries could withstand the incessant border raids which spice American labor
history. A veteran trade unionist confessed recently that
"I never recognized any jurisdiction outside of my own,
regardless where it was." [25] Tobin certainly followed this
precept in practice. Although the AFL Convention in 1909
rejected the Teamsters' claim to include chauffeurs, Tobin
nevertheless went ahead and chartered thirty local unions of
chauffeurs. The AFL then recognized his *fait accompli* and
broadened the union's name to the International Brotherhood of Teamsters, Chauffeurs, Stablemen, and Helpers.[26]

The Teamsters abandoned early any ideas that the union
should restrict itself to craft lines, despite Tobin's occasional
strictures about loosening membership qualifications. It
began organizing inside dairy employes in 1917 and em-
braced them within its jurisdiction by classifying them as
"helpers." Later it added gasoline station attendants and
parking lot employes to its growing list of eligibles. A massive jurisdictional breakthrough came in 1936 when Dave
Beck, then a Teamsters organizer on the west coast, received AFL permission to organize inland warehousemen,
as a counter-measure against the erupting CIO. Another CIO
drive served as a similar spur at Boston. The union again
changed its name, this time substituting "warehousemen"
for "stablemen." [27]

Once the jurisdictional dams were broken, there was no
stopping the flood. The excuse that the cannery workers,
represented by AFL federal locals, were in danger of being
overrun by "subversives" was enough for Beck to demand
and get an extension of jurisdiction. No longer was the
activity of another union in the field sufficient to keep the
Teamsters out. The 1947 convention had added to the
union's jurisdictional claims by including "other workers

where the security of the bargaining position of the above classification requires the organization of such other workers." With this license, Teamsters organizers could organize anything and anybody—and often did. It could serve to justify the organization of inside brewery workers (to protect the bargaining position of the brewery drivers) and of truck firm office employes. The idea that a union's jurisdiction was determined by its bargaining needs rather than its industrial classification constituted a novel approach to the question and implied the inevitable breakdown of jurisdictional boundaries. By 1961, any pretense of confining itself to jurisdictional limits was abandoned; the jurisdictional clause bluntly staked out the union's claim to "all workers, without limitation." [28]

The last may have been more an attempt to threaten the AFL-CIO rather than a genuine claim to jurisdiction, but there is little in recent Teamsters history to suggest that the union is averse to the "one big union" concept. A compilation in 1954 listed morticians and Hollywood stunt men among Teamsters members; another catalogue of Teamsters jurisdictions on the west coast included such diverse occupations as automobile salesmen, winery and distillery workers, motorcycle messengers, wholesale optical workers, frozen fish processors, vending machine repairmen, and potato chip processors. A Canadian observer listed disc jockeys at an Ontario radio station as holding Teamsters cards. The union magazine revealed election victories among such varied groups as real estate brokerage salesmen, uranium processing workers, and bowling employes. Poultry farmers in Vineland, New Jersey, organized a Teamsters local; so did dairy farmers in Saint Lawrence county, New York, and in northern Pennsylvania. "If we tried to spell out everything we have in this International Union," Hoffa told the 1961 convention, "we would have to devote almost a Sears Roebuck catalogue to it." [29]

The union has made major gains in industrial manufacturing and, under Hoffa's leadership, it has proposed full-scale organizing campaigns in public employment, mail-order department stores, and the airline transport industry. But despite its extended jurisdiction, the core of its membership continues to conform to its original jurisdiction in highway transport and intra-city drayage, supplemented by its major excursion into warehousing. The union's frequent forays beyond these boundaries have not markedly affected its basic characteristic, that of an organization that draws its strength and exerts its power from its strategic position in the center of the nation's distributive system.

2

The Convention

The leadership of the Teamsters Union draws its extensive power from the convention, held every five years. The convention, described in the constitution as "the supreme governing authority," is given "the plenary power to regulate and direct the policies, affairs, and organization of the international union." Its general duties are threefold: to elect the union's officers for the forthcoming term, to amend the basic constitution, and to determine the validity of appeals from decisions of the general executive board.[1]

Teamsters conventions are huge affairs, attracting some 2,000 delegates and as many more alternates and guests. Few cities have adequate facilities to handle conventions of this size, and both the 1957 and 1961 conventions took place in Miami Beach, Florida. As in other conventions, both of labor and non-labor organizations, the delegates often abandon their home-town inhibitions and spend freely of their generous expense allowances. But attendance at working sessions at both the 1957 and 1961 assemblies was remarkably

high, perhaps because both conventions met under the shadow of possible court intervention. Because of the legal challenge to the 1957 convention, the 1961 meeting was marked
by unusual security measures. Delegates seeking credentialed
badges ran a gauntlet of uniformed hotel police and burly
union guards, while 34 sergeants-at-arms patrolled the convention hall. The mayor of Miami Beach, invited to greet
the delegates, complained that he was stopped on three occasions, "frisked and given the third degree." Hoffa charged
before the convention began that 150 federal agents were in
Miami to investigate Teamsters affairs. During the convention, he displayed an eavesdropping device to the delegates
which he said could relay conversation for two city blocks
and cautioned them to exercise care in talking with stran-
gers. After the demonstration greeting his nomination as
president, Hoffa demanded that "every single person look
at the man sitting alongside of him to make sure that only
delegates are on this floor." The entire convention was tele-
vised at union expense to prevent any later charge that the
proceedings were falsified.[2]

The Teamsters convention originally was scheduled an-
nually, but the interim was extended to two years after
Tobin took office in 1908. In 1915, the period between conventions was stretched to five years and has remained so
since. Convention representation is based on dues payments
by local unions to the international. Intermediate subordinate bodies such as joint councils and area and state conferences also are entitled to representation by a single delegate. In addition, international officers, including executive
board members, organizers, and auditors, are given full
delegate privileges except in the election of officers. (This
latter provision, written in compliance with the Landrum-
Griffin act, forced the union's top officers, from Hoffa down,
to run in 1961 in local union elections for delegate.) Originally, each delegate represented 50 members, but the quota
was raised through the years until it reached 750 in 1952.
The 1961 convention then raised the requirement for the

first delegate from 750 to 1,000 but continued to allow additional delegates for each major fraction of 750 members over the first 1,000.[3]

As a result, some 2,111 delegates were eligible to attend the 1961 convention, but only 1,875 registered; most of the absentees were from locals too small or too distant to afford the expense. The nature of delegate representation gave effective control of the convention to the medium-sized locals with a delegate strength of from 2 to 6 delegates (equivalent to membership strength before the 1961 change of 1,125 to 4,875), while the smaller locals (one delegate representing up to 1,125 members) served as an effective counter-force. At the 1961 convention, for instance, some 387 medium-sized locals were eligible to cast 1,175 votes, or more than a convention majority. On the other hand, the 46 largest locals could cast 482 votes, or about one-fourth of the convention total, and could be balanced by the 450 small locals with one vote each. Except for those from the South, the delegates generally reflect the population trend of the country. In 1961, 757 of the eligible delegates came from the central states, 711 from the East, 528 from the West, and 115 from the South.[4]

The 1961 convention approved a significant change in the selection of delegates by local unions. It provided that all elected officers and business agents of local unions, "by virtue of such election," serve as convention delegates. If there are more elected officers and business agents than the number of delegates allotted to the local, the choice is made by the local union executive board. If there are fewer, a normal election is held to designate the additional delegates. Some delegates at the convention protested that this clause would "build a barricade around the rank-and-file to have their say at these conventions." But Hoffa spiritedly defended the clause, noting that rank-and-file members could still serve as convention delegates if they ran successfully for a local union office. In fact, the proposal was an extension of a practice Hoffa had initiated in the Central Conference of Teamsters which limited conference delegates to full-time officers and business agents. It was in line with Hoffa's concept of the union, rarely put into words, that the union's business was the prerogative of professionals. "We will be in a position to know," he told the 1961 convention, "whether or not officers who have to carry out the provisions of this constitution will be able to come here and participate." Despite the unusual nature of the proposal, it was doubtful whether it would alter normal convention representation. Even under the old rules, most of the delegates usually were local union officers or business agents, and elections merely ratified their claim to serve as delegates. But the new clause has some interesting implications. It would require international officers and organizers to maintain a link with their home local, such as a nominal office, if they wished to serve as full-fledged delegates. It would also prevent disclosure of membership dissatisfaction in the local union during the normal term of local officers.[5]

The old rules, which provided for the "selection" of delegates by a local union election or, if so authorized by a membership vote, by the local union executive board, sparked the charges of a "rigged convention" in 1957. These charges, which generated the lawsuit that brought the Board of Monitors into being, were based generally on the fact that many local unions failed to abide strictly by constitutional requirements in selecting delegates. Dave Beck exercised his vested power as union president to "interpret" the constitution by declaring the constitutional requirements "not mandatory but directory" and instructed the credentials committee to seat delegates selected "pursuant to by-laws, rules, or motions which were adopted by membership vote authorizing such method of selection." As a result, 65 delegates out of some 2,000 from 49 locals were rejected, and 50 other delegates from 42 locals withdrew from the convention. No such charges, however, could be brought against the 1961 convention. The delegates were elected under rules incorporated in a court order directing the convention;

these provided for nomination and election procedures, including distribution of campaign literature, and prompt
adjudication of appeals and protests. The union's general
executive board recommended that "where practicable" an
outside agency supervise the election, and this was done in
many cases. The 1961 delegate list thus was beyond suspicion
and constituted a definitive answer to the "rigging" charges
against the previous convention. As Beck noted, in a telegram to the 1961 convention, "this convention is made up
of the same personnel as would have been elected under the
procedure four years ago." [6]

The actual business of the convention, for all practical
purposes, is conducted by six select committees named by
the general president. These committees are rules, credentials, officers' reports, resolutions, appeals, and constitution.
The convention itself usually serves merely to ratify decisions reached earlier in committee. Before 1957, the committees consisted of small groups of five to seven members.
In both 1957 and 1961, however, all except the credentials
committee were enlarged. But even under the expanded
committee systems, less than 100 of the delegates were directly concerned with the primary decision-making power.
This does not mean that the committees function without
taking into account delegate sentiment. In 1947, for instance,
the constitution committee proposed an increase in per
capita dues from 30 to 50 cents a month. Beck, the committee chairman, later reported that "the committee has en-
deavored to inquire into the sentiment of the delegates and
has been advised that caucuses regrettably have recommended adverse action." Sometimes, delegate sentiment
serves to encourage committee action, rather than restrict
it. This occurred in 1961 when the original proposal was to
increase per capita monthly dues from 40 to 80 cents. The
proposed rise was so well received by the delegates, however,
that the committee promptly increased the dues to $1.[7]

In any case, the union's officialdom is careful not to stir
a delegate revolt by insisting upon unpopular proposals. A

dues increase, for instance, can be sweetened by coupling it with added benefits for the delegates or members. When the 30-cent monthly per capita tax was raised 10 cents in 1952, it was part of a package deal whereby strike benefits were increased from $10 to $15 a week. Similarly, the increase in per capita dues from 40 cents to $1 in 1961 was linked to three other proposals, all designed to attract delegate support. Some of the added income would be spent to raise strike benefits. In addition, the added dues would pay for a retirement plan for local union officers and employes. Then, to insure maximum support, the dues increase was made conditional upon a mandatory increase in local union dues of at least $1 a month, thus simultaneously holding out the prospect of increased local union income while guaranteeing the local union officials that they could present the higher dues to their members as a convention-ordered *fait accompli.*

Normally, the rules committee occupies itself with resubmitting a set of rules which have stayed virtually unchanged through the decades. In 1961, however, the committee proposed several rule changes, including one to prohibit rollcalls except on the election of officers, thus preventing any attempt to place the delegate on record on controversial issues. (Its immediate effect in the 1961 convention was to assure reluctant delegates that they would not have to declare themselves on the proposed dues increase and could, if they wished, tell their members back home that they had voted against it in a voice vote.) However, it should be noted that the rule it displaced was not much more democratic, since the old rule required a majority vote of the delegates to order a rollcall, reducing the minority to impotence. The rules committee report was passed without debate or dissent by the 1961 convention, since even the few but vocal anti-Hoffa delegates apparently did not attach any significance to the change.

The credentials committee, except for the 1957 convention, usually functions without controversy and presents a clerical compilation of unquestioned credentials. In 1957 it accepted Beck's "interpretation" of the constitution as a guide to its decisions. A sensitive political situation also arose in 1961 when a protest was lodged against the delegation led by Milton J. Liss, Newark, New Jersey, an opposition candidate to Hoffa. But Hoffa advised the credentials committee to ignore the protest and it did so.[8]

The committee on officers' reports theoretically has wide authority to review and deliver judgment on the accounts of their stewardship presented by the international officers. In practice, however, the committee has done little but rubber-stamp these reports. The committee on resolutions for many years confined its deliberations to inanities concerning support for the union's label program or routine acknowledgment of thanks to the convention hosts. In 1952, however, it was the vehicle by which the convention endorsed Adlai Stevenson for president. In 1961, the resolutions committee mirrored the union's increased interest in public affairs by proposing a series of resolutions on national issues, including medical care for the aged, federal aid to education, an omnibus farm bill, and automation.

A committee whose task varies with each convention is that on appeals and grievances, charged to consider protests from decisions of the general executive board. (Under the constitution, only local unions and other subordinate bodies may appeal to the convention for review; general executive board decisions affecting individual members and local union officers are final.) In 1947, the committee had 26 appeals to consider; in 1957 it had only one, and in 1961 it had none. In any case, there is no recent record of the committee overruling any decision of the general executive board, or for that matter of the convention overruling the committee.

The convention's principal committee, the committee on the constitution, has always been composed of major figures within the union. In 1952, it was headed by Beck, Tobin's heir-apparent, and in 1957 by Einar Mohn, an international vice-president who served as Beck's executive assistant. In

1961, Hoffa himself took over the chair with Harold J. Gibbons, his executive assistant, as co-chairman; five other members of the general executive board served as members. The union's constitution has undergone four extensive revisions since 1903. The 1940 revision was essentially a recodification of the previous document which had been added to, altered, and subjected to patchwork amendment for four decades. In 1952, the revision greatly increased the powers of the general president (a process initiated in 1947) and integrated the rapidly developing area and national trade conferences into the union's administrative structure. The 1957 convention, reeling under the impact of Beck's abuse of these powers, reversed the trend and stripped the general president of much of his authority. At the same time, it enhanced the power of the general secretary-treasurer and the general executive board. By 1961, the pendulum swung back and the convention again reinforced the powers of the general president, giving him almost unrestricted operating control of the union.

The 1961 revisions can best be understood in the light of their three purposes: increased centralization of the international's authority, compliance with the recently passed Landrum-Griffin Act, and a desire to strip from the constitution any verbiage which lawyers might use as a basis for lawsuits to harass the union's officialdom. The last reason loomed large, for the union considered that it had been an unjustified target for its enemies, who used all-but-forgotten constitutional provisions to hale the union into court. One of the revisions, for instance, was to delete a long section detailing the rules of order governing local meetings. When a delegate asked why the committee recommended the action, Hoffa was quick to reply: "All right, I will tell you why. We find that by having this in here, that the unscrupulous lawyers, the labor board, and everybody else who wants to create trouble for this or any other union latches onto the loose language of these provisions, and then if they find that you didn't go down through the rule book and take every single one of these orders of business, they find that you conducted an illegal meeting." [9] Some forty lawyers were in attendance at the 1961 convention and served as an informal committee to backstop constitutional changes which might eventually land the union into court.

The 1961 convention voted to pass amendments to the constitution by a majority vote, discarding a twenty-year provision requiring approval by two-thirds of the delegates. In a fast parliamentary maneuver, this provision was presented to the convention as the first order of business on the constitution and, when passed, became immediately effective. In addition, the general executive board retained its authority "to make such corrections, including the supplying or remedying of inadvertent omissions or errors, as are necessary to carry out the spirit and intent of any amendments so adopted." [10]

Amendments may be proposed by local unions, members in good standing, or the general officers, if done thirty days prior to the convention, but delegates, of course, can propose amendments during the convention sessions. Although there is no express authority for the constitution committee to meet prior to the convening of the convention, in practice the committee often is named well before the convention date. Beck noted in 1952 that the constitution committee had begun its considerations four months early, and Mohn called 1957 committee sessions in San Francisco and Washington prior to a marathon meeting in Miami before the convention opened. The 1961 committee began its deliberations June 22 with the convention still two weeks off.[11] The committee's decisions usually are kept secret until the convention gets under way, then distributed in printed form with the old constitution and proposed changes in parallel columns. This procedure stirred a flurry at the 1952 convention, when delegates protested that they were being forced into hasty consideration. Beck, the committee chairman, warned that any attempt to force pre-convention discussions of proposed changes would mean that "we will be fighting and debating the actions of this convention in the newspapers all over the country." In 1961, Hoffa apparently intended to delay distribution of the proposed changes until the committee was ready to report but changed his mind when the union's attorneys recommended that the book be distributed on the first day "so you can take it home, study it tonight, and tomorrow morning be able to digest the report." [12]

Convention proceedings, although usually quiescent and routine as delegates shout rubber-stamp "ayes" to committee proposals, can flare up into full-scale discussion on the floor —and when this happens, the international officers are less than happy. A tame, tranquil convention, not unnaturally, is regarded by the leadership as evidence of maturity and stability. Tobin made this clear when he boasted in 1920 that "this is the first time in the history of this International Union where a convention has been held in which there has been no rollcall." [13] But the convention can become unruly and turbulent, especially when the international officers misread the political signs and overstep the implicit limits which the delegates have posted. Such a convention occurred in 1940, when floor debates broke out on nine separate issues. Occasionally Tobin, an old hand at running conventions, was hard put to keep decorum. One floor outburst came when Beck, defending a constitution committee report, overran the normal ten-minute allotment for rebuttal, and a number of delegates protested when Tobin, wielding a fast gavel, passed a routine motion to grant Beck three minutes more. Tumult erupted throughout the hall as one delegate charged that Tobin "has plainly usurped the authority of the organization by stating that this vote was carried, when everybody else knows it wasn't." Tobin admonished the delegates that "if you are going to act like a lot of children, all right. (But) you must respect the rules of this convention and the decision made by the chair." The delegates refused to cease their protests and Tobin finally gave ground and sent the issue in dispute back to committee "to be redrafted." [14]

On another occasion, Tobin quieted a protesting delegate by allowing him three minutes to continue debate on an issue already resolved. The delegate was in the middle of a sentence when Tobin cut him off: "Your time is up. Sit down." Tobin then launched into a gratuitous denunciation of communism and asserted that "we will take care of any disturbers from Russia" although he admitted that "it has nothing to do with this delegate" and "I don't charge this man with anything like that." [15]

The unquestioned control exercised by the officers over convention proceedings is ensured by constitutional authority to the general president to "determine and change the order of business at the convention at any time." [16] As a result, delegates lacking administration support for their proposals often will seek compromise and agreement by maneuvering behind the scenes rather than risk an open challenge. Such a tactic was used successfully in 1952 by Lawrence Steinberg of Toledo when he sought to raise salaries of general vice-presidents from the committee recommendation of $250 to $500 a month. Two voice votes on the issue were inconclusive, and the question was referred back to committee to avoid settling it by a time-consuming rollcall. Two hours later, after a recess, Steinberg renewed his motion without committee opposition and it carried.[17] At other times, the convention has been used as a forum from which local unions can call attention to specific problems which embrace wider issues. Such a debate occurred in 1957 when locals from the National Bakery Conference proposed a constitutional amendment to protect their high-wage jurisdiction against the increase of chain store operations. It resulted in a full-dress debate, in which both sides were ably presented, and was marked by a high degree of parliamentary decorum.[18]

A spokesman for an unpopular minority must be pre-

pared to endure insults and indignities if he persists in un-
wanted debate. A delegate at the 1961 convention was
greeted with boos, catcalls, and the clamor of cowbells and
horns when he opposed the administration's proposal for
strike benefits. Peter Hoban of Chicago, who supported the
administration position, rose in protest; "I think it is grossly
unfair when a delegate is denied the right to speak his piece.
I think it is unfair that he should be booed." Hoffa, in the
chair, at first shrugged off the protest by remarking that "the
expression of friendship and comradeship takes many forms."
But he recognized the implications of Hoban's remarks and
added: "It is very unfair for a statement to be placed in the
record to say that we have not given every single individual
all of the courtesy that anybody could give. I wonder if
the delegates believe the chair hasn't bent over backwards
to create democracy in this meeting." Hoffa's statement was
greeted with applause.

Another Chicago delegate, Ray Schoessling, testified that
"I don't think I have witnessed a chairman that has allowed
more democracy to creep in here." Schoessling expressed the
impatience of the majority when he remarked that "some
people, if you would say black is white, would say white is
black for the purpose of getting into some sort of record
here." He was echoed by a San Francisco delegate who noted
that "courtesy is a two-way street" and accused the opposition of seeking "to aggrevate and agitate and create con-
troversies." [19] Hoffa apparently was especially sensitive to
any suggestion that he was not acting in the finest democratic
tradition. A California delegate, opposed to the centralization of bargaining power, inadvertently referred to "your
machine." Hoffa reacted instantly. "Stop that kind of a
remark," he shouted. "Hoffa don't have no machine. Now
strike from the record 'Hoffa's machine'." The convention
passed the motion to strike.[20]

The power of the officers, using the committee technique,
to keep the delegates from bringing an unpopular issue to
the floor is great but not unlimited. A test of this power was

narrowly avoided in 1957, when the general executive board decided beforehand to ignore the report of the AFL-CIO Ethical Practices Committee which laid the groundwork for subsequent expulsion. A request by the AFL-CIO that copies of the report be distributed among the delegates went unheeded. Under these circumstances, the only avenue open to the convention minority would have been to raise the issue by opposing the recommendations of the committee on officers reports, an unpromising prospect. But the board reversed itself in an impromptu backstage session during the convention's third day, when it decided to read the complete report to the convention and then did so without any advance notice. The convention then proceeded to strike the AFL-CIO report from the record.[21]

The innate authority of the chairman of a parliamentary body is difficult to challenge, especially when the challenger faces an unsympathetic majority. On some issues at the 1961 convention, such as the dues increase, Hoffa let the debate run freely. But his parliamentary rulings often mirrored his own feelings. For instance, a delegate arose long after a motion had been passed and other matters disposed of to ask for an explanation. "Well, you are entitled to know," Hoffa replied, "and I will tell you." On the other hand, immediately after Hoffa had declared a motion passed without taking the "No" vote, an opposition delegate protested that he had been overlooked and sought the floor on a point of special privilege. "Please be seated," Hoffa cut him off. On occasion, Hoffa let the convention be used as a sounding board to prove the widespread support he enjoyed. Melvin Angel, a foe of Hoffa from Detroit, was not a delegate but had asked for the convention floor so that he might present a resolution to allow a board of five nonmembers to serve as a tribunal of final appeal with power to remove any member from office or impound the union's treasury. Hoffa noted that Angel had not appeared before the convention committees, although he was in Miami, and then proposed its rejection. The delegates agreed unanimously. A truer test of Hoffa's clear majority came when he put the motion to adopt the amended constitution as a whole. As he asked for a rising vote, "take a stretch for a moment," he pleaded. In turn, he asked delegates standing against the walls to "squat down a minute" while taking the "No" vote. The constitution passed with five dissenting votes.[22]

Aside from the business of amending the constitution, the principal concern of the Teamsters convention is the election of officers. For many years, eligibility for office in the International Union was based on the same requirement as that for the local union—two years' past membership in continued good standing. In 1961, however, the convention raised the requirement to demand that an aspirant for office higher than that of a local union must have served for at least two years as an officer, organizer, or business agent, thus setting a minimum but loose standard of apprentice-ship training. Whatever may have been the reasons prompting this change, it had no immediate practical application since each of the current officers and any rivals all had served at least two years in some union office, as had their predecessors from the time of the union's founding.[23]

Traditionally, the election of international officers is scheduled for the final day of the convention and, under the 1961 constitution, the new officers assume office immediately following adjournment of the convention. Contested elections must be determined by rollcall, but the 1961 convention reduced to a plurality the previous requirement that a majority of all votes cast constitutes an election.[24] After Tobin's accession to power, he was unopposed for some four decades. Moreover, the long five-year period between conventions, coupled with the general president's power to fill vacancies on the general executive board, usually gave an appointed vice-president sufficient time to consolidate his political position before the next convention subjected the nomination to delegate ratification. The tradition of unopposed elections was broken in 1952, when the New York joint council sought to veto Thomas L. Hickey's candidacy for re-election for vice-president and nominated John J. O'Rourke, the council's choice. The effort failed when Beck's campaign for the presidency forced a political truce among contending factions, and Hickey was re-elected by a vote of 1,358 to 317. There was no thought in 1957 of allowing Hoffa to move unchallenged into the presidency. Four prominent delegates announced their opposing candidacies: Hickey and William A. Lee of Chicago, both fellow vice-presidents, Thomas J. Haggerty, also of Chicago, and John F. Shelley, a San Francisco congressman with a long record of AFL-CIO support. Efforts to unite on a single opposition candidate reduced the field to Lee and Haggerty, but Hoffa went on to win with an overwhelming 72.8 per cent of the vote—1,226 to 314 for Lee and 143 for Haggerty. Again, in 1961, Hoffa was challenged by Milton J. Liss of Newark, but Liss withdrew from the race when he got only 15 votes in the first 1,000 cast.[25]

Hoffa probably would have won in 1957 on his first-day strength without additional political support. But he attained his impressive majority when the Los Angeles delegation hitherto committed to Einar Mohn, Beck's executive assistant, joined the Hoffa bandwagon. The price for this support, a major inroad in the anti-Hoffa Pacific stronghold, apparently was a promise to name Mohn chairman of the Western Conference, re-elect Joseph J. Diviny from San Francisco, and elect George Mock, a general organizer from Sacramento, to the general board. An analysis of the anti-Hoffa vote in 1957 by D. W. Salmon, research director for the Central Conference of Teamsters, disclosed that Hoffa had failed to carry a majority in the New York council and faced strong opposition in key Teamsters areas like Boston and Essex county, New Jersey, as well as losing seven of the ten western joint councils. (Salmon's analysis, incidentally, credited only 189 of the 477 anti-Hoffa votes as springing from reform motives; he attributed the remainder to personal followings of anti-Hoffa leaders.)[26] By 1961, however, Hoffa's opposition was a shadow of the 1957 movement. Except for maverick dissenters, he enjoyed solid support in all areas of the country and had almost universal backing. Some of this support, especially from the west coast, may have been reluctant and reflected the artificial unity forced on the union by the Board of Monitors which had made Hoffa a symbol of solidarity. But the election revealed clearly that Hoffa had used his presidential powers to consolidate and expand his political fortunes.

Despite Hoffa's undoubted popularity in 1961, his followers took no chances and ran a "scare" campaign to whip up support. On election day, the convention hall looked like a gay circus carnival as delegates, many attired in candy-striped jackets with straw hats to match, wearing giant-sized "Hoffa" re-election buttons, snake danced through the aisles to the accompaniment of a jazz band, bongo drums, and tooting auto horns. The cost for these circus trappings, incidentally, came from a fund amassed by individual contributions of $25 from many of the union's 3,000 organizers and business agents. The enthusiasm of the delegates spilled over into the hotel lobbies and streets; even the skies above Miami Beach's shoreline carried a "re-elect Hoffa" streamer sailing behind a cruising plane.[27]

3

The General President

Daniel Tobin was general president of the International Brotherhood of Teamsters from 1907 until 1952, although by 1947 he had abandoned much of the daily routine. Tobin's long regime was based on a simple political strategy: dissipate the possibility of revolt by the larger locals by never threatening their independence. Tobin served as a kind of constitutional monarch and carefully kept from violating the tacit boundaries of his office. As a result, the organization he developed was a loose federation of individual satrapies rather than the monolithic empire so often described.

Dave Beck, who took over administrative command of the union in 1947 as Tobin's executive vice-president and succeeded to the presidency in 1952 after Tobin's retirement, quickly discovered that much of the general president's impressive constitutional powers did not exist except on paper. As executive vice-president, Beck chafed under Tobin's veto, but once he donned the constitutional mantle of general president he made a serious attempt to implement his constitutional authority. Beck struck hard in 1953 at the heart of the New York organization, second only to Chicago's as an independent dominion, in an effort to assert the international's authority. But Beck lacked the courage to carry the fight through and soon retired to the counting house where he contented himself with manipulating the union's growing treasury. Like Tobin, Beck virtually abdicated his office before he retired; more and more, he left the daily routine to Einar Mohn in the Washington headquarters and to men like Frank Brewster on the west coast and James R. Hoffa in the midwest.

While Beck played "banker and broker" and preened himself as the union's ambassador to the nation and the world, Hoffa quickly consolidated his leadership in the midwest and moved southward and westward. Hoffa recognized (as Beck apparently did not) that true political power within the Teamsters could derive only from strength in collective bargaining, the union's *raison d'etre*. He used contract negotiations to cement locals with common economic interests into strong, cohesive political units. After Hoffa assumed the general presidency in 1958, he continued along these lines in the Western Conference and along the Atlantic coast. The 1961 convention provided Hoffa with an opportunity to implement his strategy with constitutional mandates, and he emerged with greater authority than that given either Tobin or Beck. Exile from the AFL-CIO forced the Teamsters into serious political activity and separate alliances with other internationals, both AFL-CIO and independent. These in turn required a centralized international authority, thus emphasizing again Hoffa's demand for power. Under Hoffa, the Teamsters Union gradually lost its federated look and, despite occasional assertions to independence by local leaders, its president became the vigorous leader its constitution said he was.

The three men—Tobin, Beck, and Hoffa—had little in common despite superficial similarities. All three were born in poverty and each climbed the rungs of the Horatio Alger ladder to personal wealth and fame. Like so many other American union leaders, they scaled the heights impelled by colossal ambition and unaided by the benefits of formal education. But they came out of diverse generations, and each left a separate stamp on the union. Tobin was a labor leader of the Sam Gompers school—indeed, he had entered the union movement as a member of the Knights of Labor. Tobin's concept of unionism was narrowed by the blinders of craft jurisdiction, and he never quite adjusted himself to the realities of the New Deal labor movement with national perspective and power. He conceived of his influence as derived from individual capacity, rather than from the organized economic power of his union. Beck, however, recognized union power for the political lever it was. If he was unable to wield it fully, it was because he regarded its source as the net worth on the balance sheet rather than the union's bargaining strength. Beck was a product of the "get-rich-quick" boom of the 1920's. He never lost his appetite for the praise of the business community and once boasted that his personal income-tax bracket was so high that the government had a greater stake than he did in the $50,000 annual salary of the Teamsters president. Beck fell in prestige and power when he tripped over some of his own financial booby traps—an incident of dramatic irony. Hoffa also is obsessed with an apparent desire for money, and his record is replete with instances of strange borrowings from associates and friends, of questionable business enterprises and inexplicable cash transactions. But unlike Beck, Hoffa evidences no great urge to parade as a paragon of business enterprise, nor is there much indication that he has sought to amass wealth for its own sake. To Hoffa, a product of the depression 1930's, money represents security and power rather than prestige and glory.

It was these three men—Tobin, a garrulous, petty ruler who was satisfied with the semblance of power instead of its substance; Beck, an ambitious, vain prima donna who sought the plaudits of financial princes above that of his own members; Hoffa, a power-driven turbulent overlord whose record bespeaks ruthlessness and loyalty, underworld connections and intellectual alliances—who have made the office of Teamsters president what it is today.

A discussion of the extensive powers granted to the general president by the Teamsters constitution must necessarily run the full gamut of the union's operations, and many of these will be discussed elsewhere in relation to other areas of union administration. The constitution summarizes these powers by providing that "the general president shall have general supervision over the affairs of the International Union . . . subject at all times to review and approval of the general executive board." [1] The board's power to pass on the president's conduct was dropped in 1947 when Beck's star was on the rise and reinserted ten years later, coincident with Beck's fall. It is worth noting that this power of review was left intact when the 1961 convention restored presidential supremacy. For many years the constitution required that the president "shall devote his entire time" to his duties, except in case of "a call to service by the government." The clause was meaningless. Tobin took frequent excursions outside the formal limits of union office to serve as labor chairman of the Democratic national campaigns, Beck devoted much of his time to his own tangled business affairs, and Hoffa insisted on continuing as chairman of the Central Conference and president of his own local union. The 1961 convention bowed to realism when it gave express permission for general officers to hold office and serve subordinate bodies. [2]

The general president is granted judicial authority "to interpret the constitution and laws of the international union, and to decide all questions of law thereunder between meetings of the general executive board." He also is given the power "to settle and determine all grievances and disputes submitted to him by joint councils, local unions, and other subordinate bodies, or members" in the interim between board meetings. [3] The provision limiting the exercise of these powers to periods when the board was not sitting was inserted by the 1957 convention, as was the proviso that the president must report his judicial opinions, if appealed, to the board "for its approval, reversal, or modification." The clause significantly does not require such reports where no formal appeal is taken, although the ruling conceivably could set a precedent for future decisions.

The presidential perquisites are as generous as the annual salary of $75,000 a year, plus "all expenses." The constitution sanctions unlimited travel allowances for the president "for the purpose of promoting the interests and welfare of the international union and the making of diplomatic contacts with other organizations and for the purpose of conserving his health." He also may "take periodic rests" and, "in his discretion, travel in this country or, with the approval of the general executive board, abroad." Specific allowance is made for "the full and complete maintenance of his wife so that she can accompany the general president." [4] These generous travel provisions were written into the constitution in 1940, subject to a rider that they applied "only to the present incumbent of the office of general president," that is, Tobin. But the rider was removed when Tobin was succeeded by Beck. The constitution, as amended in 1961, also contains authority for the board to provide "such accommodations by purchase, lease, or otherwise, as it believes desirable for the housing of officers and employes while on official union business." But long before the constitutional authority was granted, the international in 1942 bought the Tobins a $45,000 home, outfitted with $10,000 worth of furnishings, in Miami Beach, Florida, for use as a winter residence. Four years later, it built a summer home for him on the oceanfront near Marshfield, Massachusetts. The generosity was continued even after Tobin's death, and the 1957 Convention authorized his widow to make continued use of the Massachusetts property "for the remainder of her lifetime," with the union paying for upkeep and operation. [5]

Beck kept his residence in Seattle and arranged to have

the union purchase his home from him at an appraised price of $163,000. He then occupied it rent-free with the union paying for maintenance and taxes. Hoffa so far has made no attempt to follow the examples of his predecessors and he continues to own his modest, if comfortable, home in Detroit. But he successfully urged the 1961 Convention to raise the president's salary from $50,000 to $75,000 to make the post the highest paid in the labor movement. In addition, the union pays his expenses while he is in Washington, his headquarters, as elsewhere; in 1960, the union reported to the Labor Department, it paid out $17,081 for Hoffa's expenses.[6]

Tobin had set the fashion for generous salaries for president; he had assumed office at $150 a month and, although always making a show of reluctance, induced later conventions to raise it until he got $40,000 a year in 1940, then $50,000 in 1952. Tobin was a shrewd political operator, whether in the AFL or the national Democratic Party, but he ran his union office as if the Teamsters were the same organization he had nurtured before World War II. During his 45 years as union president, he maintained a loosely run, one-man organization, exercising what power he dared from behind an old-fashioned roll-top desk in the union's Indianapolis headquarters. Tobin regarded himself not so much as the general of a militant army but as the kindly "Uncle Dan" of his locals and members. He freely dispensed advice on all manners of subjects, not excluding medical, as editor of the *Teamsters Journal,* and filled its columns with moral strictures. But as far as internal union administration was concerned, Tobin asked only that the locals pay their dues on time and not disturb him unduly with demands for international intervention and payment of strike benefits. He was highly regarded for his personal honesty, but he did not dare lance the boils of corruption and racketeering which festered under his administration and sorely tried his successors. It took the machine-gun assassination of an international vice-president and the wounding of a general organizer to bring Tobin into Chicago in 1932, but all he did was stamp his approval on a plan already worked out by public officials and he made no real effort to clean up the mess.

Tobin's true relationship to the powerful local leaders was illustrated by his failure to secure convention approval for a project long dear to his heart—creation of a death benefit fund for the union's members. Tobin's desire for such a fund may have come from envy of his fellow AFL presidents who could boast of the millions they had amassed in similar ventures. But he also knew that such a fund would strengthen the bond between the international and the individual member and thus could reduce the power of a local leadership to defy the international. "For twenty-three years," Tobin declared in 1930, "I have been preaching the doctrine of establishing a death benefit. We have lost union after union because we had nothing in the way of benefits or insurance to offer them." [7] But the very reasons Tobin wanted such a fund served to cool any enthusiasm for it on the part of local leaders. Moreover, many locals had developed their own death funds and saw no gain in paying out of their treasuries for parallel benefits from the International. The establishment of Old Age and Survivors Insurance under the New Deal, of course, removed much of Tobin's argument for the fund and it soon became a dead issue.

Beck never enjoyed Tobin's popularity with local leaders, probably because they were suspicious that he might make good his oft-repeated threat to transform the loose federation into a centralized organization. While he was on the west coast as a general organizer, Beck had built by 1947 a membership of 226,000 members, or more than one-fourth of the national membership. Much of this gain could be attributed to his use of the conference principle in union affairs —the association of varied local unions in area-wide and industry-wide conferences to seek greater uniformity in bargaining practice. When Beck came to Indianapolis in 1948 to serve Tobin as executive vice-president, he must have been appalled. In contrast to the International's shabby quarters, his own Seattle office had been a smartly furnished model of efficiency, including ever-clicking teletypes with direct connections to other Pacific coast cities. Beck was a great admirer of the arts and science of big business. "I run this place just like a business," he told an interviewer in 1938, "—just like the Standard Oil Company or the Northern Pacific railway. Our business is selling labor. We use businesslike methods." A decade later, he reiterated this theme with significant overtones for a labor leader committed to the democratic process: "Unions are big business. Why should truck drivers and bottle washers be allowed to make big decisions affecting union policy? Would any corporation allow it?" [8] Beck's leadership as executive vice-president spurred the union into an aggressive campaign which raised its membership from 890,000 to 1,120,000 by 1952, and he submitted his claim to the general presidency.

Beck made sure of election at the 1952 convention when he secured Hoffa's support by expanding the executive board, backing Hoffa's candidacy for one of the two vacancies, and agreeing to let Hoffa head the still unformed Central Conference of Teamsters. Beck tried to assert his authority with vigor, promised "immediate plans for a thorough investigation" at the slightest indication "of the possibility of misappropriation of funds," and placed a number of locals in which misconduct was suspected under trusteeship.[9] But he had no stomach for the certain fight which these steps would initiate within the union and soon backed off. His retreat became obvious within a year when he allowed Hoffa, a comparative stranger in the east, to shoulder aside Thomas Hickey, a Beck vice-president, during crucial negotiations in the New York trucking industry. Beck's failure to protect Hickey, his spokesman for reform, was observed with suspicion by informed observers. A. H. Raskin, the *New York Times* labor reporter, suggested that the real significance of Hickey's ouster was "the altered role in which it casts Dave Beck," and John Herling, a syndicated labor

columnist, bluntly reported from Washington that Hoffa
had taken over the *de facto* leadership of the union.[10]

Beck's power and reputation diminished rapidly thereafter. It vanished completely when he fled to Europe on
"urgent business" when the Senate committee began looking
into his affairs, then hid behind the fifth amendment after
his return. Beck's refusal to testify left unchallenged a
multitude of allegations concerning misuse of authority in
his personal financial dealings, including a charge that re-
payment of some $300,000 to the Seattle joint council
represented restitution of funds taken without authority
rather than the return of "borrowed" money. It is worth
noting that Beck defended himself specifically on only one
of the numerous committee charges when he appeared before
the 1952 Convention—the charge that he had profited personally from investments he had supervised for Mrs. Ray
Leheney, the widow of a close friend and associate. "God
knows I tell the truth," he vowed as he told the delegates he
never knew he had gained a $4,700 profit in investing a
$83,000 fund he had helped raise.[11] Beck's defense before
the union as to the other charges was to assail the committee
as "a one-way street" and to explain that his difficulties arose
"because I have been in a high income tax bracket due to
my international salary and my being successful in investment" and therefore had shifted investment opportunities
to his son or friends.

Beck's downfall was Hoffa's opportunity, and Hoffa
promptly took advantage of it. The fact that his full name is
James Riddle Hoffa has prompted some observers to remark
that his middle name (taken from the Irish maiden name
of his mother) well describes his personality. The riddle
presented by Hoffa lies in the contrast between his unchallenged skill at collective bargaining and his admitted underworld associations; of his apparent hunger for money, especially in the form of cash, and his austere, modest pattern of
personal living; of his cynical appraisal of the motives of men
with his declaration that "every man has a price," and his

reliance for internal administration upon such men as Harold Gibbons, whose home local in St. Louis has been acclaimed as an international showplace of union democracy.

Hoffa grew up the hard way. Born in 1913, he was orphaned at the age of seven when his father died, a victim of coal-dust poisoning; he quit school after the ninth grade to take a job as a department store stockboy, then a grocery warehouse worker. With four friends on the job, he organized his first strike. "It lasted less than an hour," he boasted later, "because we timed it right. We went on strike just as a load of strawberries came in. Management had to get the strawberries unloaded before they spoiled." Organizing a union in Detroit in the early thirties was rough going. "The police would beat your brains in for even talking union," he recalled. "There was only one way to survive—fight back. And we used to slug it out on the streets." Hoffa first organized the grocery workers into an AFL federal labor union, then sought a Teamsters charter. He was given a debt-ridden local, amalgamated it with another local in equally poor shape, and began his climb.[12]

There are as many unexplained facets in Hoffa's early union career as there are in his latter-day dealings. The amalgamation of the two unions did not automatically make Hoffa, then 20 years old, the union's head; the title was held by Owen (Bert) Brennan, Local 299's business agent. But by 1935, Brennan had left the local to become business agent for the joint council in Detroit, and two years later Hoffa was elected Local 299 president. Hoffa's first major objective was organizing the car-hauling drivers, a campaign which gave him a sense of national perspective which contrasted with the narrow local outlook of other Teamsters business agents. He put his ideas into practice when he established one of the first national trade conferences in the union, the haulaway industry, and used it later as the model for similar groups throughout the Teamsters structure. Meanwhile, his outstanding abilities as a negotiator brought him to the chairmanship of the Central States Drivers Council bargaining team by 1940 and, two years later, he formed the Michigan Conference of Teamsters. By this time Hoffa was a seasoned veteran of 29.

Hoffa's political acumen matched his ambition. He used his position within the Central States Drivers Council to cement alliances with locals in other states and to begin the building of a personal machine based not only on friendship but service. "No one ever calls for assistance from Jimmy Hoffa," Harold Gibbons later remarked, "but that he gets it in full and complete measure." [13] Tobin recognized Hoffa's growing influence in 1948 when he named the 35-year-old rough-and-tumble organizer to a vacant trusteeship in the International Union. Four years later, Hoffa showed up at the 1952 convention with a bloc of votes big enough to force his election as vice-president. Beck's debacle provided him with the push upward toward the presidency.

Hoffa's strength within the union rests squarely upon his record as a negotiator. Perhaps his greatest bargaining achievement came in 1955 when he headed a union team which established the principle of wage uniformity in a 12-state area. After he became president, he used his abilities as a union negotiator to enhance his political position on the west coast and along the Atlantic seaboard. Hoffa often cites these economic achievements to confound his critics. "All this hocus pocus about racketeers and crooks," he once told his home local, "is a smokescreen to carry you back to the days when they could drop you in the scrap heap like they do a worn-out truck." [14]

Hoffa could dismiss the nation's concern about the Senate committee's disclosures as "hocus-pocus," but he could not ignore the fact that this concern was at the root of the popular outcry against him and the union. His own early record is mixed. He has a long record of police arrests, but most of these came as a result of picket-line scuffles and are the hash-marks of any active labor organizer. He also was the target of two indictments relating to less praiseworthy trade union practices. One involved a venture by Hoffa to "organize" the proprietors of family-owned, family-operated grocery stores, and the other was an attempt to regulate competition in the Detroit waste-handling market. Hoffa pleaded *nolo contendere* to the latter charge while the grocery indictment, at first extortion, was reduced to a misdemeanor. Hoffa was found guilty and put on probation, complying with an order to refund some $7,500 in dues to the grocery storekeepers. (It is doubtful whether the practice of enrolling family-business proprietors within union ranks is extortion *per se* since a number of unions, including the Teamsters, have a long tradition of owner-operator membership. But it is true, nevertheless, that labor racketeers often use picket-line sanctions to enforce compulsory union membership for proprietors without offering in return even the superficial benefits of a commercial association.) In 1953, an unfriendly congressional investigation, headed by Representative Wint Smith (Rep., Kans.), put the national spotlight on Hoffa's personal affairs, disclosing complex business relationships with an array of racketeers and hoodlums. One of the more sensational committee revelations was the disclosure that Hoffa and his union ally, Bert Brennan, had used their wives' names to set up a truck-leasing firm which supplied equipment for a large auto haulaway concern and had reaped a 15-fold return within four years from a $4,000 investment.[15]

Hoffa met strong opposition from within the union on his way to the top. It stemmed from more than a desire to keep the union's reputation free of taint, and it was more than a natural effort to stop the rise of a strong leader. Hoffa's insistence that the union's collective bargaining goals could be reached only through nationwide trucking and warehouse agreements which cut across local and regional lines was unpopular with many local business agents who did not look forward to future roles as dues collectors and grievance adjustors. The anti-Hoffa group on the general executive board, led by Frank Brewster, chairman of the Western Conference of Teamsters, decided upon a show-

down at the board's meeting in March, 1956. The group
was prepared to use the issue of a Hoffa-sponsored loan to
the discredited International Association of Longshoremen
and confidently counted six of the thirteen votes on their side
while giving Hoffa only two—his and John O'Brien's of Chicago. But Beck, never one to precipitate an internal battle,
stymied the strategy by refusing to put the issue to a vote,
giving the Detroiter a crucial victory in his intra-union relationships.[16]

But as Hoffa's power and influence grew, so did his attrac-
tiveness as a target—especially for the Senate committee
which began its extensive probe into union racketeering
early in 1957. The committee followed through on the earlier
revelations of the House investigators. It soon added an impressive list of charges of its own, including the sponsorship
of racket-run paper locals to swing a New York joint council
election, payment of legal fees out of union treasuries to
defend union leaders accused of racketeering, the use by
Hoffa of his union position to promote a Florida real estate
development and secure favorable bank loans, the employment of hoodlums with long criminal records. Some of the
testimony which damaged Hoffa most, at least from a trade
union point of view, described acts which were clearly legal
but which outraged normal labor ethics. One of these disclosed that two business agents of Hoffa's home local, Zig-
mont Snyder and Lawrence Welch, operated a nonunion
auto wash which paid wages as low as $1 a day. The com-
mittee probed deeply into the affairs of Hoffa's home Local
299 and those of Local 337, run by his close friend Owen
(Bert) Brennan. It amassed considerable evidence that
Hoffa and his colleagues were involved in numerous con-
flict-of-interest situations and left little doubt that Hoffa
and Brennan, with the abject compliance of the local executive boards, manipulated the union treasuries without restraint.[17]

A favorite committee target was the Central States, Southeast and Southwest Areas Health and Welfare Fund, which

administers a massive health and hospitalization plan covering more than 100,000 union members. The choice of Union Casualty and Life Insurance Company as carrier for both the Central States Fund and the smaller Michigan Conference of Teamsters Health and Welfare Fund had attracted the attention of congressional probers in 1953 and again in 1956. But the McClellan committee subjected the two funds to intensive and searching investigation and committee staff members spent an aggregate six man-months on the task.[18] Much of the testimony centered on the relationship between Hoffa and Paul Dorfman, whom the committee called "a major figure in the Chicago underworld." The committee charged that "the evidence is clear that Hoffa used these two funds to pay off a long outstanding debt to the Chicago underworld." [19] This was done, according to the committee, by channeling the insurance collusively to Union Casualty, although it was not low bidder, because Union Casualty's agent was an agency owned by Allen and Rose Dorfman, the son and wife of Paul. As a result, the committee disclosed, the Dorfmans collected more than $3,000,000 in commissions and service fees over a nine-year period. More than half of the commission and fee payments, the committee insisted, were excessive and constituted "a milking of funds." [20]

Insurance statistics are complex and do not lend themselves easily to a layman's understanding. The Northeastern Life Insurance Company of New York, Union Casualty's successor company, presented a lengthy memorandum to the committee defending the award, and the committee staff prepared a rebuttal. A careful reading of these documents, as well as the testimony and findings of the committee, makes it clear that there undoubtedly was favoritism in the initial award to Union Casualty and in continuing the contract over the years. However, it is less certain that the union members, who were the fund beneficiaries, suffered from the transaction. The Northeastern Life memorandum argued that, although the proposed retention fee (the percentage of premiums retained by the company to cover its expenses and profit over and above the claims paid out) was initially set at 17.5 per cent, actual experience over an eight-year period reduced this to an average 7.6 per cent. It admitted that commissions to the Dorfman agency were twice the normal rate but insisted that these commissions were charged to the fund at a standard rate, with the company paying the excess amounts from profits earned in other phases of its business. The reason for paying excess commissions, it added, was to finance the Dorfman agency "in its formative years." The staff reply dismissed this argument as "ludicrous" but did not challenge the statistics cited by the company.[21]

Whatever the proper interpretation of these facts may be, there is little question that a "very strange and peculiar relationship," as Robert Kennedy, the committee counsel, termed it, existed between Hoffa and the Dorfmans. Both Paul and Allen were often seen at various Teamsters meetings, and they were partners with Hoffa in a number of business ventures including a girl's camp, an oil company, and various real estate promotions. Moreover, even after Northeastern Life terminated the Dorfman agency contracts, it arranged for the agency to continue to receive $500,000 a year in service fees and vested commissions. "I had the feeling," the Northeastern Life president told the committee, "that the company would lose this business if the Dorfmans were cut off."[22]

Shortly after the McClellan hearings got under way, Hoffa was accused of "hiring" a Senate committee investigator as an attorney—an episode marked by cloak-and-dagger meetings in taxicabs and open parks. He was quickly indicted for bribery but, with the same fortune which attended other government attempts to jail him, was acquitted.

Hoffa used his acquittal on the bribery charge as the springboard for the plunge into the race for the Teamsters presidency. Within days after he was freed, he announced his candidacy at a Chicago meeting of his supporters. In connection with this announcement, Hoffa proposed a nine-point platform which deserves consideration as one of the few instances in which he put his union philosophy in written form. He proposed more extensive use of international union funds to underwrite collective bargaining strategy, remarking that "the International is not a banking institution," and urged support for his oft-repeated goals of "area and national contracts" with strike benefits to be paid for recognition and sympathy strikes as well as primary contract disputes. As an "immediate, realistic goal," he suggested a 2,000,000-member union, with the International setting aside one-fourth of its income as a minimum budget for organization. The union's research department should be expanded, he added, and the Teamsters should co-operate with the AFL-CIO and other unions in joint campaigns, "providing there is recognition of our jurisdiction and reciprocity of cooperation."

Hoffa specifically endorsed the AFL-CIO codes of ethical practice in such areas as democratic process, union finances, local union charters, health and welfare funds, racketeering, and conflicts of interest, excepting only the AFL-CIO prohibition which barred union officials from pleading the fifth amendment. Hoffa who personally never used the constitutional provision although he often relied on what one exasperated senator called "the best forgettery of anyone I have ever known," cited a United States Supreme Court opinion that use of the privilege cannot justify an attempt "to discredit or convict a person who asserts it." [23]

It was a platform good enough to win him election at the 1957 convention, and his record of performance on these pledges ensured his re-election in 1961. Both votes constituted rejection by the delegates of the principal contention of his detractors that he is unfit to serve as union president. Nevertheless, the allegations against him, especially those of the Senate committee, merit review if we are to understand the nature of his leadership. The Senate charges against Hoffa centered around three general indictments: alleged misuse of union funds, toleration and support of crooks and racketeers within the union, and improper relations with employers under union contract.[24] It would require a separate volume to make a proper assessment of the committee's case against Hoffa. Often the committee was as unfair to him in its hunger for headlines as he was to it in his recurrent "forgettery" and his constant evasion of questions. Some of the committee's inquiries went far afield, as in the case of labor violence in Tennessee where it centered its attention on events which had little to do with labor corruption. Nevertheless, it amassed a mountain of testimony which demanded answers which were never given, explanations which were never offered.

Some of the testimony dealing with Hoffa's personal financial affairs, notably his frequent transactions in cash and his disdain for normal banking procedures, as well as the use of union funds to secure financial advantages for himself and his friends, raise serious moral issues. But many of these facts were made public as early as 1953 and have been available both to members of Hoffa's home local and to the Teamsters generally. "To Hoffa," one observer remarked, "almost all of society is peopled by businessmen looking to make a fast buck;"[25] apparently, this attitude is shared by Hoffa's supporters, who look upon his appetite for cash as a natural attribute of the acquisitive society.

The committee built a strong case against Hoffa for his failure to keep a promise to purge the Teamsters Union of underworld characters who have infiltrated its ranks, although it should be noted that this condition antedated Hoffa's rise to power. The testimony seems incontrovertible that Hoffa has shown an unusual and strange tolerance for men with criminal records and hoodlums with reputations which would bar them from decent society. Some of this failure to act can be explained away by the realization that even the extensive powers of the general president are restricted by the realities of union politics. It is also true that the refusal of Hoffa's detractors to discriminate among his supporters and efforts to smear all Teamsters with the same brush have only served to unite all the accused, guilty and innocent alike, in a defensive alliance. But it is significant that, unlike Dave Beck (who was as eloquent as any preacher in his denunciation of racketeering before his own fall from on high), Hoffa has not only tolerated racketeers but has consistently refused to denounce them. Many of the persons identified before the committee as hoodlums and racketeers never were connected with the Teamsters Union and a number of those identified with union affairs have long since dropped out of sight. But it is true, nevertheless, that Hoffa often has gone beyond mere tolerance in his relationships with such men. He has been on intimate personal terms with them, attended testimonial dinners in their honor, and backed them in their quest for high union office. There is a tendency within the Teamsters, even among Hoffa's opponents, to excuse these relationships as growing out of friendship. "I think the greatest mistake Hoffa ever made," Milton J. Liss, who ran against Hoffa for president in 1961, remarked, "is being overloyal to some of his friends who took advantage of him." [26]

During its final year, the committee concentrated its barrage against Hoffa in the crucial field of employer relationships. Hoffa himself had flung the challenge in the fall of 1958: "Why don't the investigators inspect the product where it really counts—the wages and conditions under which our members work?" [27] Accordingly the committee prepared to show in 1959 that Hoffa had "entered into collusive arrangements by which contract terms were arbitrarily abrogated or watered down to a degree that left them virtually meaningless." [28] It was a difficult field which the committee entered, and one unsuited for the researches of amateurs in industrial relations. Among the hundreds of contracts with which Hoffa was concerned, the committee's investigation came up with a bare handful which were questionable either in drafting or administration, Hoffa himself readily admitted that he had agreed to change some contract provisions "to meet the changing of times and the salvation of an employer who would have gone out of business." "It is not our duty as union officers," he added, "to put companies out of business and displace our members out of work." [29] The problem of judgment arises because it is difficult for the outsider to distinguish between labor statesmanship and mendacity; the two opposites often use identical techniques. "The exact line of demarcation between 'sweetheart' contracts and the exercise of labor statesmanship is not readily drawn," George W. Taylor once remarked. "Any labor agreement is likely to be construed as unsatisfactory—or worse—by individual employes or groups of employes." [30] Without definitive information, the observer is forced to conclude that here, as in the case of union finances, the final verdict must be rendered by Teamsters members themselves.

The committee dismissed Hoffa's testimony as "a curious and practically unfathomable mixture of ambiguity, verbosity, audacity, and mendacity" and made no secret of its belief that Hoffa, although declining to use the fifth amendment himself, nevertheless encouraged his principal associates to do so. "It looks as if they are protecting you," a senator told Hoffa. Some of Hoffa's evasive answers can be attributed to his fear of an unjustified perjury indictment. "All they need are two persons who say you're a liar and you're on trial for perjury," he once explained, "and how often can you be lucky?" [31] But it is noteworthy that Hoffa met charges of employer payoffs and bribery forthrightly and without the slightest evasion. "I will tell you that is a lie," he shouted when Robert Kennedy charged that income listed in his tax returns as gambling profits actually came from employer payoffs. In a similar vein, he asserted his innocence at the 1961 convention. "I stand here," he told the delegates, "and look you in the eye, each and every one of you, and say I have never sold out a worker in my life, never." [32]

Hoffa served his first term as a "provisional" general president subject to the supervision of a three-man Board of Monitors appointed by United States District Judge F. Dickinson Letts. The establishment of the outside board to oversee his administration was written into a consent decree which settled a federal suit brought by some New York members to challenge the legality of the 1957 convention. After a cooperative beginning, the relationship between the union and the Board of Monitors quickly deteriorated to constant squabbling and prolonged litigation, especially after Martin F. O'Donoghue, the board's chairman, made it clear that he was determined to oust Hoffa from the presidency. The entire affair ended in a fiasco when O'Donoghue resigned and the court was unable to secure a successor. Finally, after more than three years, Letts authorized the union to call a special convention, which promptly re-elected Hoffa.[33]

The key to Hoffa's popularity among his fellow Teamsters lies in his single-minded dedication to spending almost all his waking hours in the union's vineyards. At the Washington headquarters or on the road, he is on the long-distance telephone continually, settling major and minor problems with quick, off-the-cuff decisions. He seems unable or afraid to delegate authority and, although he heads a union of 1,700,000 members, he still insists upon participating in the daily routine of his home local in Detroit. Throughout the 1961 convention, he never let go of the chairman's gavel, except during the period when he was being re-nominated and re-elected. "Personal contact," he once told a study group at American University, "is the key to service; giving the membership service is the only reason we are in business." He will often delay his exit from a union meeting to listen to a member's grievances and announce his decision on the spot. "Whenever there's a strike and they want me, I go," he has said. "I like this job," he told an interviewer on another occasion, "every hour I work here is an hour of pleasure." He pushes himself at a man-killing pace. In 1961, he began the year by participating in the marathon Central States contract negotiations. Then he served as chairman of the New England wage talks; he followed through by heading the over-the-road and local cartage negotiations in the western states, overriding some local objections. Conscious of the political weaknesses displayed by Tobin and Beck because they removed themselves from the hurly-burly of wage negotiations, Hoffa apparently is determined to remain active in all phases of the union's life. "I am a working president," he once boasted.[34]

Hoffa's personal future is clouded by the incessant efforts of law officials, especially the federal Department of Justice, to convict him of some crime. He was acquitted in two federal trials, both arising out of situations investigated by the Senate committee, and is facing a third indictment at this writing—a charge of conspiracy to commit fraud in connection with the development of a Florida real estate project. In addition, his tax records are under continual review, and there is little doubt that any conviction of the Teamsters president would be a feather in the cap of the successful prosecutor. If this were to occur, one of its immediate results—if the conviction were for any of the twelve crimes listed in the Landrum-Griffin law—would be Hoffa's ouster from office. And even if it were a lesser crime, it still might bring forth demands that Hoffa be dropped as unfit for office. In these circumstances, the 1961 convention passed a carefully written resolution, taking cognizance of the many charges against Hoffa and specifically listing the Florida land deal, his refusal to remove leaders accused of racketeering, and "accusatory implications" that he had conspired to destroy telephone records sought by the Senate committee. The resolution then proclaimed that "we are the judges of the conduct of these officers" and went on to give "its wholehearted ratification and approbation of all of the activities and conduct of the general president and other officers and employes during their service (with) this International Union." The resolution passed without dissent.[35]

Hoffa lives a Spartan life, rejecting whiskey and tobacco and worrying continually about his diet. He added some ten pounds to his muscular frame during the 1961 series of negotiations, and this fact seemed to concern him almost as much as reports of a membership revolt in Cincinnati. Indeed, one of the few changes he has made in the luxurious headquarters Dave Beck built in Washington has been to install a steam room, complete with masseur, parallel bars, and calisthenics equipment. "Hoffa trains as strenuously as a prize fighter," an observer noted. He is subject to flashes of quick temper and, although he has learned to keep his feelings under control when in public, occasionally finds himself resorting to bare fists when aroused. In Detroit, he enjoys the reputation of a warm, attentive family man and, until his wife began to accompany him on his incessant traveling, he often flew home to spend week ends with her and the children. His daughter, a Phi Beta Kappa student at college, taught school before she married; his son, an all-state football star in high school, is studying law. Hoffa revealed some of his family pride during his acceptance speech at the 1961 convention. "My daughter finished college," he told the delegates. "It is the first generation for either a Hoffa or Poszywak, my wife's family, on her mother's, her father's, my mother's, and my father's side to have had an opportunity to complete college. It is a great American institution that permits men like myself from a warehouse to here, my wife from a laundry to where she stands here today." But his real enjoyment of life is concentrated in the union he has served (and which has served him) since he reached nineteen. One reason, perhaps, for his insistence that no problem is too minute for his personal attention is an almost obsessive fear that he may lose contact with the ordinary member. "I have had experience with general presidents who have lost touch with local union affairs," he once explained. "I have no desire to forget where I came from." John English, the union's secretary-treasurer, gave Hoffa the ultimate plaudit when he declared that "when it comes to work, Jimmy Hoffa surpasses them all." [36]

4

The Officers

In contrast to the extensive powers of the president, the domain of the general secretary-treasurer of the Teamsters Union is limited. "The secretary-treasurer's job," Tobin told the 1947 convention, "is nothing more than that of a top bookkeeper." [1] Tobin was only a little less than fair in his interpretation. Until 1957, the secretary-treasurer had little authority even within his own office, and one of the few responsibilities he could exercise without the approval of either the president or the general board was the quarterly designation of the password, a relic of the days when unions were secret orders. Tobin made his disparaging remarks when he tried to cut the secretary-treasurer's salary from $30,000 to $20,000 a year, to distinguish more clearly between the presidency and the less-exalted secretary-treasurership. The 1947 convention turned Tobin down, but in 1961 the delegates left the secretary-treasurer's salary at $50,000 a year when they hiked Hoffa's to $75,000. Before 1957, the secretary-treasurer had little authority over investments or the meaningful handling of union funds. Indeed, he did not even have the power to hire his own assistants. It was a measure of the job's insignificance that Beck turned it down when Tobin offered it to him in 1946.[2] Tobin then named John F. English, a former Boston coal wagon driver who had been a general organizer since 1936. English, whose birth in 1889 makes him the oldest member of the union's executive board, fitted Tobin's job description well since his service as a general organizer had emphasized internal auditing of local union accounts.

English's appointment as secretary-treasurer coincided with the rise of Dave Beck to national power and resulted in an unhappy personal decade for English, who resented Beck's free-wheeling operations. English indicated his frustration in 1957 when he pleaded with the convention to "give us a constitution where it won't be a one-man organization and 'you do as I say or else'." [3] The personal feud between Beck and English became public knowledge in 1956 when English refused to cosign a check reimbursing Beck for the furniture in the president's Seattle home, despite specific executive board authorization for such an expenditure. English was a member of the union's three-man finance committee but was unable to veto Beck's general investment policies which he regarded with suspicion. Within his own office, English was hampered by a relatively narrow conception of his duties, a result of his long tour of duty as a local auditor. He placed great emphasis upon efficient administration and regarded obedience to form as fulfilling constitutional requirements, although form often camouflaged serious errors of substance. For instance, he insisted that proof of the financial fidelity of local union officers lay in the fact that auditors had discovered only $500,000 in delinquent per capita taxes over a twenty-two-year period. It apparently did not occur to him that prompt payment of per capita tax could not absolve a local secretary-treasurer of financial irregularities in other respects.[4]

The effectiveness of the auditing procedures which English

regarded so highly is open to question. In 1957, English reported that the union's three auditors (actually, general organizers with auditing duties) had examined the books of 969 local unions, collecting some $95,000 in underpaid taxes, over the five-year period between conventions.[5] But the purpose of the audit was not to uncover anything except the local union's ability to meet its per capita obligations. "We don't give what you would call a regular audit," he explained to the Senate committee. "We have the auditors go over the books and find out whether the organization is going ahead or going backward. If we find out that the expenses are more than the receipts, we call them to task." After some sparring with committee members, the following revealing colloquy occurred:

THE CHAIRMAN: Mr. English, the primary purpose of that audit is to determine whether the local union has been remitting to the International the proper amount of per capita dues or tax.
MR. ENGLISH: Yes, sir.
THE CHAIRMAN: This regular audit is not designed and is not of such a nature as would disclose or reveal to you that there might be considerable money being expended improperly. It does not reveal that?
MR. ENGLISH: It does not.[6]

The constitution requires that the books of all subordinate bodies, such as local unions or joint councils, be audited at least once a year by a certified or chartered public accountant. In addition, the general secretary-treasurer is empowered to appoint international auditors, with salaries and privileges equal to those of general organizers.[7] The latter practice was instituted in 1957 and grew out of the previous arrangement by which general organizers, appointed by the president, were given auditing responsibilities under the secretary-treasurer's supervision. Their number is determined by the executive board, and recently has been set at three. The international auditors are authorized to audit local union accounts at least once between conventions but this requirement can be fulfilled if the general executive board directs a certified public audit. Copies of all audits and all financial statements required by law must also be forwarded to the secretary-treasurer.

The 1957 constitution also spelled out in great detail the duties and powers of the secretary-treasurer, enlarging on a more general description in the earlier laws. He was named custodian of all assets, charged with the conduct of all financial correspondence, instructed to preserve the union's archives and keep minutes of executive board meetings. A significant change in 1957 provided that the secretary-treasurer's signature, "as a ministerial act," be required on all investment documents, thus giving him a potential veto power on the union's investment policies. Another 1957 change gave formal recognition to the previous practice of distributing the convention's verbatim proceedings to each delegate, and board minutes to each vice-president.[8]

The union keeps a sizable cash balance on hand—the consolidated balance sheet as of June 30, 1961, showed almost $3,000,000 available, divided between a checking and a savings account.[9] Strict controls govern the issuance of checks. "No less than seven individuals," English reported, "share the responsibility of drawing a check. It would be utterly fantastic even to conceive of a misappropriation occurring." Neither the president nor secretary-treasurer has blank checks available nor are checks signed in blank. Instead, the blanks are kept in the custody of a disburser who is held accountable for their use.[10] A survey of the union's bookkeeping procedures in 1958 by the firm of Price, Waterhouse and Company, made at the direction of the Board of Monitors, resulted in general approval of English's office, except for its failure to establish adequate records of dues payments by individual members. The inspection, according to the accounting firm, disclosed that the International did not maintain "complete authoritative records of membership or of members in good standing" and that summary reports of such data by local union secretary-treasurers, submitted in accord with a constitutional mandate, were "not reviewed for accuracy or completeness" nor were they "incorporated into formal records." It recommended maintenance of a name-by-name record of dues payments which would enable the International Union to keep tighter control over per capita tax obligations, provide a basis for regulating payment of strike benefits, and allow an independent check of the dues eligibility of candidates for office and convention delegates.[11] The firm's conclusions, accepted by a majority of the Board of Monitors, were rejected by the union, which asserted that the proposed revision of its record-keeping system would cost $1,500,000 for installation and increase record-keeping costs by over $142,000 a year.[12]

English agreed to modify the reporting form used by local unions to allow summaries to be compiled by electronic accounting machines which many local unions already had installed. This served to prevent the possibility of error, by chance or design, on the part of the local secretary-treasurer. However, it did not achieve the declared goals of the Monitors to establish the member-by-member dues-recording system which English had insisted was a wasteful duplicate of local-level records. The new procedures, English declared, "represent only minor modifications and constitute a vindication of procedures in effect since 1947." [13] But the significance of the dispute is much greater than the relative efficiency of two accounting systems. The very looseness of the union's record-keeping procedures at international headquarters contradicts the popular conception of the Teamsters Union as a monolithic organization with absolute control at top levels. Indeed, the inability of the international headquarters to determine independently the qualifications of its members or, for that matter, even who its members are, illustrates the reliance it must place upon cooperation from local union officers.

Another function of the secretary-treasurer's office is the granting of charters to local unions. For years, this was a relatively routine operation. But disclosures by the Senate committee that English's office had perfunctorily issued charters to seven "paper locals" in New York, at Hoffa's request

and without prior notification to the New York joint council, brought demands for more careful issuance of such charters. The 1957 convention, accordingly, required that charter
applications bear the signatures of seven members "employed within the jurisdiction of the International Union,"
receive the approval of the secretary of the joint council
involved, and be approved by the president, secretary-
treasurer, and the general executive board. These procedures
were made somewhat looser by the 1961 convention which
took away the veto power exercised by the joint council,
reducing its function to a nonbinding indication of approval
or disapproval. The 1961 convention also approved the
granting of charters, "upon such terms and under such conditions as the general executive board shall consider appropriate," to locals with an unlimited geographic jurisdiction.
Another change in charter procedures ordered by the 1957
convention was the explicit declaration that issuance of a
charter to a local union "is in no way conditional upon the
affiliation or nonaffiliation of the International Union with
any other organization"—a legal stratagem to counter any
claim by a seceding local that disaffiliation with the AFL-
CIO constituted a breach of contract and thus voided any
constitutional clause designed to prevent secession.[14]

The 1961 constitution requires the secretary-treasurer to
issue an annual financial report, supported by a certified
public audit, to be published in the union's monthly journal.[15] The requirement for financial disclosure has been in
the constitution since 1903 but, until 1957, there had been
no formal provision for periodic reporting. In practice, the
secretary-treasurer issued quarterly financial reports to all
local unions and published comprehensive accumulated
totals in his reports to conventions. The 1957 convention
provided for semi-annual reports to be published in the
journal; this was changed to annual reports in 1961.

The union's total net worth, as of December 31, 1961, was
$37,722,805, a loss of some $800,000 since 1957. The total
does not include some $5,500,000 in a separately funded

retirement plan for employees of the International Union. The huge treasury is the result not only of the tremendous growth in union membership after 1935 but of careful husbandry of constantly accruing assets through the years when income invariably exceeded expenditures. The merger of the original unions in 1903 found the cupboard almost bare, with a treasury of $25,000 for a membership of 32,000—or an individual equity of 80 cents a member. The value of the individual equity has see-sawed through the years, as the organizing drought of the 1920's paradoxically strengthened the relative position of the union's treasury and the cost of organization and strikes during the New Deal years weakened it. But the total net worth of the organization has shown a steady and almost spectacular growth, reaching its peak in 1957 at $38,503,000, with an individual equity of $27.30. Because of heavy organizational expenditures and strike benefit payments under Hoffa the total dipped slightly, but a dues increase passed by the 1961 convention was designed to renew the upward spiral.

The International relies substantially on dues income. In 1960, it reported total receipts of $9,158,187; of this sum, some $7,106,839 (or 77 per cent) came from per capita dues, $1,209,842 from investments, $720,711 from its share of initiation fees, and $120,174 from sale of supplies.[16] As we have seen, this was not enough to balance expenditures and Hoffa asked the 1961 convention to raise the monthly dues from 40 cents to $1. A brochure distributed among the delegates noted that the 40-cent tax was the lowest of any international union in the labor movement, and that the dollar's buying power had shrunk since 1952 when the 40 cents was voted. More persuasive than logical argument was a proposal to earmark 22 cents of the dues increase to establish a retirement system for local union officers, including most of the delegates. At the same time, a convention decree raising dues in each local by $1 a month not only offered hard-pressed local union officers a way to meet the increased per capita tax without chancing a membership referendum but also

promised them an immediate 40-cent-per-member dues increase for local purposes. The convention argued the issue
at some length but passed the proposal overwhelmingly.[17]
The higher dues, given the 1960 average dues-paying membership of 1,480,000, would raise annual income by more
than $10,500,000 and, even with some $4,000,000 earmarked
for the pension system, easily erase the operating deficit. The
convention also voted to increase the International's share
of local initiation fees from $1 to $2.5, adding another million dollars to its annual revenue. On the basis of 1960
experience, the higher income would increase the union's
net worth by more than $6,000,000 a year.

Except for the cash on deposit in banks and an inventory
of local union supplies, the bulk of the union's total assets,
as of June 30, 1961, was concentrated in investment securities of $29,621,029 and some $5,000,000 in real estate.[18] The
investment program has been in existence since 1915 when
the convention gave the executive board authority to invest
excess union funds, above a $200,000 cash cushion, "in first-
class bonds, either national, state, or municipal." In 1929,
attracted by the paper fortunes recorded daily in Wall Street
dispatches, Tobin proposed to invest some $2,000,000 in
union funds "in reliable bonds and stocks of first-class, sound
corporations." "The selling and buying of money," Tobin
said, "is purely a cold-blooded business proposition." The
convention gave Tobin the authority he wanted and established a finance committee, composed of the president, the
secretary-treasurer, and a third member, with instructions
to invest union funds in excess of $500,000. But the abrupt
decline of the stock market and the beginning of the depression robbed Tobin of the courage of his financial convictions, and the union's money remained invested in safe, if
unexciting, government securities.[19]

The finance committee, despite its constitutional authority, functioned as a rubber stamp for the president's decision.
Tobin confessed as much in 1952 when he told the convention: "The general president has almost complete charge of

all investments, subject only to the approval of the general executive board. The general secretary-treasurer collects the money and puts it into the bank." [20] Accordingly, Beck took over personal responsibility for the union's assets when he assumed office in December, 1952. The fact that some $18,-700,000 was invested in governmental securities, earning only a minimal interest, while $7,400,000 lay idle in bank deposits, horrified Beck's highly developed sense of financial propriety, and he promptly set about to alter this situation. Beck first invested the ready cash, most of which had been in noninterest-bearing bank accounts or drawing 1½ per cent interest. His next target was the government bonds which the union had acquired during the war years at 2½ per cent interest—"too little," he noted, "to make up for depreciation in the purchasing power of the principal." The market price of the government securities had fallen since purchase, but this fact did not deter him. He disposed of $12,000,000 worth at a substantial discount—as much as 13 per cent off face value—and prepared to sell the remainder for reinvestment in "safe and socially productive investments." [21]

Beck distributed the investments in three areas—mortgage loans to affiliates and employes, conventional mortgage loans, and government-insured Veteran Administration mortgage loans. The 1961 convention report by the secretary-treasurer disclosed that $16,487,000, or 55 per cent of some $30,000,000 in investments, were in veteran mortgages, with $7,400,000 more in government bonds and notes. The rest was deposited in conventional mortgages, including loans to affiliates, principally joint councils and local unions seeking to construct their own buildings. English reported with evident satisfaction that the union's investments were doing well; "the ratio of delinquencies in our mortgages," he explained, "is less than the national average and the interest return is 3.8 per cent." In 1960, income from investments, less financial expense, totaled $1,209,852—a handy sum when it came to balancing the operating deficit.[22]

Beck, an old hand at financial legerdemain, followed a common business practice in maintaining a relatively low cash balance, relying on the organization's ability to borrow funds for emergency needs at a lower rate of interest than it was getting from long-range investments. A series of strikes in the spring of 1957 forced bank borrowing when the union's normal income could not meet benefit payments which ranged as high as $67,500 a week. Beck then arranged with a Seattle bank for a $850,000 loan, but the strikes continued and the union's cash balance dwindled to $158,909 by June 30, 1957. Beck continued borrowing from the bank, pledging the investment securities as collateral. But Beck's practices provoked an outcry within the union. The spectacle of one of the nation's richest unions, with a net worth of $38,000,000, running to the banks for loans to pay off current expenses did not sit well with Beck's colleagues, less sophisticated than he in the way of the money bazaars. Many union leaders came from home backgrounds where borrowing money was a confession of poverty, and they resented the implications for their union. Rumors began to circulate within the union that Beck's financial policies had placed the organization in financial peril.

Beck explained in vain that the union's investment reserves were sound collateral for bank loans and his practices were saving the union money. The attacks continued and Beck glowered on the platform at the 1957 convention while English, with ill-concealed glee, accused Beck of "over-committing the International" and failing to keep a sufficient cash reserve. Beck took the floor in self defense with a remark that "it is easy to be a Monday morning quarterback." He explained patiently that the invested funds were yielding higher returns than the union paid in interest on its borrowed money. He went on to lecture the convention on the vagaries of the bond and security markets, noting that there was a current vogue to shift from veterans' mortgages to more lucrative financing. "I welcome your talking it over with your banker," he assured the convention delegates, "and discussing it with them, or other people who have a thorough understanding of finance." [23]

The convention listened sympathetically to English's plea that the president's wide authority over investments be cut sharply. It raised the number of board members on the finance committee from three to seven and provided that at least five must constitute a quorum; it also gave the executive board authority to remove any committee member by majority vote. Instead of the $500,000 cash cushion of the Tobin era, the secretary-treasurer was instructed to keep at least 25 per cent of the union's funds (aside from fixed assets such as real estate or furniture) in interest-bearing bank accounts or short-term government obligations. Another change cut from 6 to 3 per cent the share of the union's treasury which could be advanced to other labor organizations "for the maintenance, protection and preservation of the labor movement"—but the higher limit had never been approached since it was set in 1947, and the 3 per cent share made available more than a million dollars for such loans.[24]

The constitution provides, in addition to a semiannual audit by a certified public accountant, for a similar survey by the three elected trustees. The survey of the union's accounting practices made by Price, Waterhouse and Company described the trustees' audit as an amateurish performance and urged the union to place more reliance upon the certified public audit. The tradition of electing member-trustees to review the secretary-treasurer's accounts is an old and venerated practice among labor unions, whatever its failings as a true review. Each of the three trustees is paid $7,200 a year for his semi-annual service and the job is widely regarded as a steppingstone to higher union office. Hoffa was a trustee before becoming vice-president in 1952, and John W. Backhus of Philadelphia served in a similar capacity before he became a vice-president in 1957. The affairs of two of the three present trustees, Ray Cohen of Philadelphia and Frank J. Matula, Jr., of Los Angeles, came under the scrutiny of the Senate committee; the third, John Rohrich of

Cleveland, was nominated for re-election in 1957, by Louis (Babe) Triscaro, another committee target. (Indeed, Matula performed his auditing duties in 1960 only by courtesy of a "freedom break" from the Los Angeles county jail where he was serving a sentence for perjury.)[25]

Both the general president and general secretary-treasurer serve on the general executive board, along with thirteen vice-presidents. The size of the board has grown from the seven-man group Tobin took over in 1907 to its present fifteen as a result of political pressures from regional leaders. At one time in the 1957 convention, Hoffa was prepared to enlarge it to nineteen, but the momentum of the Hoffa bandwagon made additional patronage unnecessary. A seat on the board is a lucrative plum; vice-presidents who are not full-time organizers receive a salary of $12,000 a year (raised from $6,000 in 1961), plus an additional stipend if the general president assigns them specific duties.

We have noted that the 1957 convention, sensitive about Beck's use of presidential authority, gave the board considerable power to checkmate the general president. The 1961 convention returned many of the presidential prerogatives, especially those concerned with operating authority. But the board retained most of its policy-setting powers, including the right to supervise the issuance of charters, review the president's judicial opinions, decide basic issues such as affiliation or merger, and guide the policy of the union's monthly magazine.[26] In practice, of course, the board's authority is meaningful only if it is exercised. Under the 1961 constitution, five of the board members (the president, the secretary-treasurer, and four vice-presidents appointed as area directors) automatically became employes of the International Union. In addition, the general president is authorized to name an executive assistant (who has been a vice-president since the practice was instituted in 1947) and can, if he wishes, hire other vice-presidents as general organizers. Thus, nine of the fifteen board members elected in 1961 were on the union's payroll and, except for English, dependent on Hoffa for their jobs. Hoffa did not need this union-paid majority, it should be noted. Of the six others, two had been appointed by Hoffa to the board and two others were on Hoffa's slate in 1957. It was not always this way. Although two of Tobin's board members also served as general organizers, English had resigned his board post when named a general organizer, in accord with a tacit requirement that the board be governed by local chieftains rather than international employes.

For years, election of the general executive board was as cut and dried as the re-election of Tobin himself. The board was virtually self-perpetuating; as an old-timer would retire or die, Tobin would name his successor. This resulted in a board weighted with age, and in 1947 three of its members had more than 35 years of board service. But death and politics quickly changed the balance, and by 1961 only English and John T. O'Brien of Chicago had more than a decade's tenure. The 1961 board had an average age of about 55. Even more impressive was the comparative youth of the union's principal leaders, except for English. Hoffa was 48; Gibbons, his executive assistant, 51; Einar Mohn, Western Conference director, 55; Thomas E. Flynn, Eastern Conference director, 55, and Murray W. Miller, Southern Conference director, 46.

The constitution directs that the officers of the International Union shall "as near as practicable, be uniformly distributed throughout the entire country." In addition, the 1961 convention limited any state to one vice-president, subject to a "grandfather clause" which insured the continued eligibility of any sitting board member.[27] Under this rule, the east coast has six members (including English), the central area five (including Hoffa), the west three, and the south one. The distribution is proportionate to the concentration of union membership in each area. Although there is no constitutional mandate for this purpose, the geographic dispersion is maintained in case of a member's death by appointing his successor from the same area. Thus, John J. Conlin of Hoboken, New Jersey, was succeeded by Anthony Provenzano, and Owen B. Brennan of Detroit was succeeded by Frank E. Fitzsimmons of that city. The vice-presidents are numbered from first to thirteenth, "in accordance with their seniority on the general executive board," as directed by the constitution.[28] The addition of eight new vice-presidents by the 1957 convention presented some difficulties, since a person's rank as vice-president might well presage his union future. The issue was settled by ranking them in accord with their membership tenure within the union with John J. O'Rourke, who joined in 1917, as sixth vice-president, and Gibbons, who had merged a former CIO warehouse union into the Teamsters in 1949, as thirteenth.

Except for the general organizers, vice-presidents in the Tobin and Beck regimes had few responsibilities when they were not attending board meetings. In many cases, of course, the mere holding of the office of vice-president was sufficient to make one's influence felt, but it was not unusual for a general organizer to override a vice-president's authority, as Carl Keul of Des Moines did to Sidney L. Brennan in 1956.[29] All this changed under Hoffa, who handed out territorial assignments to each vice-president at the first board meeting after he took over. "For the first time in our union's history," Hoffa announced, "the international vice-presidents will have authority outside of the executive board meetings. It will be the responsibility (of each vice-president) to stay on top of all situations which might develop in his territory. Locals will report their difficulties directly to him." More detailed instructions were outlined in two letters from Hoffa to the joint councils and local unions. The vice-president in each area, they were told, would watch negotiations and strikes, keep informed of all legal actions against any local union, mediate disputes between the membership and a local union officer "to avoid unnecessary filing of charges," settle jurisdictional disputes without formal joint council action, help protect locals from raids by other unions, and assist trade division progress and organization. "This new program in no way," the letter added, "alters the relationship of the local unions to the joint councils." [30]

Until 1952, the Constitution provided that the first vice-president would succeed to the union's leadership if the general president died or resigned in office. However, the seniority system usually made the first vice-president an aging crown-prince, often older than the king himself. Hoffa's first vice-president was O'Brien, 17 years his senior. The 1952 convention gave the board power to name the president's successor, but the 1957 constitution altered this to provide for a special convention within 60 days, with the first vice-president serving in the interim. This was again changed in 1961 to allow the board to name the interim president if it should decide that the first vice-president, "because of physical infirmity," is incapable of acting as president.[31] The board also may call a special convention of the union, with power to establish its rules and procedures, by a two-thirds majority.[32]

The board, by constitutional grant, is given "such powers, duties, and authority as are not otherwise delegated to the general president and general secretary-treasurer" and is regarded as the "governing authority" over the union. It must meet at least quarterly and, upon the written request of a majority, can hold special meetings within 30 days.[33] Under Tobin, the board met only twice a year, usually a winter meeting in the South and a fall meeting to coincide with the AFL annual convention. Beck followed Tobin's practice until 1957 when the impact of the Senate investigations forced a total of 13 board meetings during 1957. The constitution permits action by the general executive board when it is not in formal session "by telegram, letter, or long distance telephone." [34] This technique was first permitted by the 1940 constitution, but during the Beck regime there were constant complaints that he had substituted telephone balloting for formal meetings. On occasion, Beck did not even poll the full board but called only enough members to attain his majority and then put the proposal into effect—

even though some members of the board did not even know it was under consideration.[35] The 1957 convention plugged this loophole by requiring that any board action by telephone should be in the form of a multi-phone conference call and that "all members of the general executive board shall be polled and the action of each individual member shall be made known to the remaining members of the general executive board."

During Hoffa's first term, the continuing attack on Hoffa and the union by the Senate Committee, the Department of Justice, and the Board of Monitors forced an artificial unity upon the board. Despite this, however, there is little question that the composition of the board lends itself to division which should become more evident if the attack subsides. Some board members, like O'Rourke and O'Brien, are products of a school of unionism which has little time for theory and less for idealism. Their personal associations, the committee hearings made clear, are in great measure tied to underworld characters, men in the uneasy shadows of the sports world, and the "fixers" of a corrupt business environment. On the other hand, Gibbons is a former Socialist and a fervent believer in membership participation in union affairs, an intellectual who finds in unionism a constant challenge and gratification. Likewise, Mohn is a forward-looking, serious unionist who is not frightened by new ideas or nonconformist proposals. (It is worth noting that Gibbons and Mohn were tagged by Hoffa and Beck, respectively, to serve as executive assistants to the president.) Hoffa apparently has a natural inclination to side with the O'Rourke-O'Brien group but he also has an evident respect for intellectuals like Gibbons and Mohn. When and if a division shows itself among the board, Hoffa will have to decide whether he will serve as mediator or arbiter. There is little to suggest that Hoffa enjoys a peace-making role, and much to suggest that Hoffa will simply declare his position and overwhelm any opposition. Whichever side he chooses finally, it will serve to underline his dominant role in the union.

5

The Staff

The ability of a general president to make extensive use of his wide powers, even when he is as intense and strong an individual as is James Hoffa, depends upon the quality of his staff. The members of the general executive board, as we have seen, serve as Hoffa's principal lieutenants, with specific geographic responsibilities. At the headquarters level, Hoffa's chief aid is Harold Gibbons, his executive assistant. Because Hoffa is reluctant to surrender his authority to decide even minor matters of policy, Gibbons does not enjoy as much decision-making power as was exercised by Einar Mohn, who served as Beck's assistant, or by Beck himself, who virtually ruled the union when he was executive vice-president. Gibbons does exercise considerable independence in settling issues which fall within well-defined limits of policy, although "diplomatic" matters involving relations with other unions are referred to Hoffa even where policy is relatively clear. More important, Gibbons, a man of imagination and vision, has constant access to the president's office and often is able to persuade Hoffa to pioneer in previously uncharted areas.

Two other men also serve part time in a personal relationship to Hoffa—Joseph Konowe, who carries the title of administrative assistant, and Lawrence Steinberg of Toledo, Hoffa's personal representative. Konowe, who heads a large merchandising local in New York, comes to Washington to act as emergency backstop when both Hoffa and Gibbons are out of the city. Steinberg, who also served as Beck's personal representative, is based in Toledo and is an experienced trouble shooter who is assigned special responsibilities in difficult areas of internal problems. (It should be noted, however, that Hoffa often acts as his own trouble shooter, especially where there is a conflict between elected local union officers and the membership.)

All three men—Gibbons, Konowe, and Steinberg—are relative newcomers within the Teamsters. With a common background from the CIO, they represent a point of view which regards the union as a social force within the community, ready to assert itself at civic and political levels as well as at the bargaining table. It is a point of view alien to many of the old-line business agents and, despite their proven loyalty to the Teamsters, the three often are regarded with misgivings by their colleagues. As if to offset the implications of such a "kitchen cabinet," Hoffa maintains close political and personal relations with union leaders who resent the Gibbons group. His office is a frequent host to visiting Teamsters who represent a more narrow outlook on union goals, especially to some union officials whom the Senate committee accused of unethical practices. Moreover, one of Hoffa's closest associates in Washington is William Bufalino of Detroit, whom the committee accused of practicing "a most disgraceful type of unionism." [1] Bufalino, who also is an attorney, was Hoffa's choice as the union member of the Board of Monitors despite widespread opposition within the union, and he was credited by Hoffa with nullifying the monitors' opposition to a new convention.[2]

Unlike many international unions with many fewer members, the Teamsters Union does not have a large staff of general organizers or international representatives. The union had but four organizers on the International's payroll in 1925 and only fourteen (including four whose duties were limited to auditing local books) in 1940 when the membership was approaching the half-million mark. Beck raised the number to 30, including three auditors. In its 1960 financial report required under the Landrum-Griffin law, the union listed 22 general organizers, including three vice-presidents with that title, and three general auditors. As the personal choice of the general president, the organizer's first loyalty is to the administration. During Tobin's regime, an organizer was certain of a lifetime job—"from now until perpetuity," as a delegate complained in 1930.[3] But neither Beck nor Hoffa gave such guarantees. After his assumption of office, Hoffa dropped five general organizers hired by Beck, including Beck's son and Beck's nephew. A sixth Beck organizer, Dan Tobin's son, Fred A. Tobin, continued to fulfill legal and legislative functions but lost the title. Hoffa clearly indicated his patronage concept of the office when he replaced Thomas Hickey, a defeated vice-president who had opposed him for election, with Hickey's old foe, John O'Rourke, as general organizer in New York.

As noted, O'Rourke, Joseph Diviny, and George Mock each serve as both vice-president and general organizer. In addition, three general organizers, Harold Thirion, Thomas Owens, and William Griffin, head national trade divisions and two others, Ralph M. Dixon and Robert Graham, are assigned to conference duties. Francis J. Murtha of Chicago, another general organizer, is executive secretary of the Central States, Southeast, and Southwest Area Pension and Welfare Funds and also serves as executive secretary for the Central States Drivers Council. Most of the other organizers are assigned to geographic responsibilities and at least two of them, John M. Annand of Los Angeles and Ray Schoessling of Chicago, also serve as presidents of their home joint councils. Two men, Frank Brewster of Seattle and Jack Gold-berger of San Francisco, are listed on the payroll as special organizers, apparently with part-time duties.[4]

Almost all of the general organizers have risen from Teamsters ranks, usually after a demanding apprenticeship in local or regional staff positions. "We have the youngest staff of representatives in the country," Hoffa once boasted. "We know what we want and we're not afraid to go out and work to get it." [5] Few of them actually participate in routine organization campaigns. They are essentially staff assistants to the general president and are used to strengthen slipping locals, coordinate crucial negotiations or strike situations, administer trusteeships, or mediate internal dissatisfaction with a local leadership. They are handsomely paid for their services, as are other employes. Gibbons received a salary of $30,000 in 1960, Mohn, Western Conference chairman, $30,-000, and Thomas E. Flynn and Murray W. Miller, who head the Eastern and Southern Conferences, respectively, $26,000 each. The three vice-president organizers each received some $20,000 for the year, and so did 16 of the general organizers. Salaries for the other organizers ranged from $15,000 to $20,000. William T. Mullenholz, who acts as English's top assistant as comptroller, received $22,500. Samuel Baron, field director of the national warehouse division, received $16,000, Fred Tobin, legislative representative, $20,000, and Abraham Weiss, research director, $15,500. The union's constitution traditionally has set high maximum salaries, but Tobin and Beck always reserved the top paying jobs for their favorites. The 1957 convention, which stripped the general president of much of his authority, ordered that all organizers with three years' experience be paid the maximum, set at $20,000. But the 1961 convention returned the power of setting actual salaries to the general president, keeping the maximum at $20,000.

All officers and organizers, except the general president and general secretary-treasurer who have unlimited expense accounts, also get $7.50 a day for "incidental expenses"—a tidy sum of $2,720 a year for which they are accountable only to the Internal Revenue Department. They also are allowed $200 a month for automobile expenses and $25 a day for hotel and other costs in addition to transportation when they are away from their homes. The 1960 financial report listed an additional $20,000 a year in allowances and expenses for Hoffa and a similar sum for Gibbons. Five other officers received $10,000 or more in allowance-expense reimbursements for 1960; so did twelve other members of the staff.

These salaries and allowances apply only to officers and employes on the payroll of the International Union. There is no available study of salaries for the 3,000 full-time officers and organizers who carry on most of the union's administration and organization activities. Personal observation suggests that few of the regional or local organizations can match the generous salaries paid by the international, but that most are set at an adequate $10,000 to $12,000 a year. There are exceptions, of course. The Senate investigation disclosed salaries for some local officers at $25,000 and $30,-000 a year. The peak was undoubtedly reached by Chicago Local 710, of which vice-president John T. O'Brien is secretary-treasurer. The committee disclosed that Local 710's officers, in addition to their regular salaries, were splitting a one-third commission on dues paid by the local's 14,000 members—a $150,000 prize in 1958. O'Brien himself was paid $11,700 in salary plus $47,289 in commissions and bonuses from his local union, in addition to what he received from the International; in 1960, the International paid him $12,316 in salary and allowances.[6]

An organization not directly affiliated with the Teamsters but which has drawn most of its members and finances from Teamsters ranks is "Labor's Minute Men." Directed by Gibbons, it is ostensibly a form of self-insurance among union business agents who may be prosecuted for activities arising out of their union duties. The organization is financed by an initial membership fee of $1,000 from each member, plus $60 annual dues, and its seven-man board is given wide latitude in spending its resources. It was formed shortly after the 1957 Teamsters convention but lay dormant until late in 1960 when Gibbons revived it; during the 1961 convention, it conducted an energetic campaign for members among the delegates. The principal purpose of "Labor's Minute Men," as outlined in its membership brochure, is "to furnish counsel and expert assistance of all kinds to persons or organizations who need it by virtue of their involvement in the cause of organized labor." But its list of purposes also seeks "to promote the influence within organized labor of those individuals deemed to be best qualified to achieve a program for labor"—a thinly disguised proposal for intra-union caucuses within the Teamsters and other labor organizations. It originally had a goal of 1,000 members, which would establish a $1,000,000 treasury plus $60,000 in annual dues. Membership is open to any member of organized labor, subject to the approval of the board, but most of its members appear to be Teamsters officials.[7]

The Teamsters Union conducts an extensive research program, both at the international level and among subordinate organizations. Its research director is Abraham Weiss, a well-known economist with statistical experience in several federal agencies. A research workshop held in December, 1957, attracted 18 research directors from various conferences, joint councils, and local unions, most of them professional economists or statisticians. The international's research efforts were initiated in 1941 by David Kaplan, who had been economist for the International Association of Machinists. Kaplan's efforts to establish proper research facilities were frustrated by Tobin's lack of interest in the project, and he never developed the department to its full potential. Weiss has had more enthusiastic backing from Hoffa, but he has been hampered by the failure of many locals to submit bargaining contracts, despite a constitutional requirement. The department functions primarily in the collection and analysis of data to assist in contract negotiations. It also publishes occasional surveys of comparable Teamsters contract clauses within a multi-plant national company, such as an elaborate analysis in 1959 of contracts held by Teamsters locals in 55 bargaining units of the General Electric Company. Weiss and Sidney Zagri, who heads the union's department of legislation and political education, appear occasionally before congressional committees considering legislation affecting the trucking industry; other appearances are made at hearings of the Interstate Commerce Commission or government regulatory agencies. One of the research department's responsibilities is supervision of a small but adequate library in international headquarters. It includes files of some 120 periodicals, mainly labor and trade journals, some 200 books, principally of labor interest, proceedings of government hearings, and bound volumes of the union's own magazine and convention reports.

One of the lesser responsibilities of the research department is to coordinate educational projects sponsored by area or local units, but the International itself does not conduct a full-fledged educational program. Some locals, like Local 688 in St. Louis, operate well-staffed schools and training institutions, and many others use facilities offered by university extension services. A proposal which attracted some attention in 1958 concerned an offer by some Detroit locals, including Hoffa's own Local 299, to buy a $150,000 Lake Michigan estate for use as a training school for business agents. The proposal was described by the Senate committee as a device to provide funds for Paul DeLucia, a notorious Chicago gangster. It was revived in 1961 when the Central Conference voted to purchase the estate for a similar use.[8] Another area where the international has lagged in providing services for local unions or its members is in its failure to establish a technical department, common in other unions, which would provide assistance in job engineering problems or help negotiate welfare and pension plans. Similarly, the 1961 convention refused to establish a separate civil rights department, although it passed a resolution supporting "attainment of civil rights and equality of job opportunity." [9]

One ancillary area where the international union is well staffed is in the field of legal assistance, as the $771,369 item for "legal fees and expenses" in its 1960 financial report testifies. Edward Bennett Williams holds the title of general counsel, but he has centered most of his efforts on the problems presented by the courts and the Board of Monitors in the long battle to depose Hoffa. Significant labor cases are handled by David Previant of Milwaukee and Herbert Thatcher of Washington, both distinguished labor attorneys. Edward Wheeler, another lawyer, specializes in cases before the Interstate Commerce Commission. Florian J. Bartosic is the union's "house counsel," charged with maintaining a docket of all Teamsters litigation and collecting a library of pertinent briefs, memoranda, and decisions, as well as with normal legal duties. Another lawyer, Fred E. Tobin, who functions primarily at the intra-union level, screens local union bylaws before they are passed upon by the general president and supervises all internal appellate procedures and establishment of trusteeships. Lawyers who serve the international plus some one hundred attorneys counseling subordinate bodies have established the National Conference of Teamsters Lawyers, an extra-union body which meets annually to discuss the intricacies of legal problems. One of the principal obligations of the attorneys, aside from the actual defense of the union's interests before courts or government agencies, is to explain current labor law in layman's language. When congress passed the Landrum-Griffin act, for instance, Hoffa called a special meeting of joint council officials in Washington where the attorneys, led by Previant, conducted a three-day short course in the new law. Similarly, the lawyers appeared at a meeting of the general board in 1961 to discuss eight recent decisions by the national labor relations board as well as a number of cases, decided and pending, before federal courts.[10]

Hoffa has a deep distrust of newspapers and newspapermen, and regards public relations as a necessary evil forced by the continuing attacks on the union. His dislike for the press often borders upon hysteria, especially when editorials accuse him of being a dictator or when they attempt to influence union affairs. "It is none of your business," he once told an interviewer who referred to attempts to depose him. "(Whether Hoffa) should be president of the International Union isn't a question that concerns you or your newspaper." He applied the touchstone of the dollar to decide the value of a newspaperman at the 1961 convention—"the intellectual brains of the newspapers," he chortled, "work for wages less than truck drivers." He once linked the enmity of the press to the influence of advertisers and described the principle of press freedom as "payola with a constitutional guarantee." [11] Under these circumstances, it is something of a tribute to the power of the press that the International spent $306,955 during 1960 for public relations.

Until 1961, the public relations department (which includes responsibility for editing the union's magazine) was directed by John McCarthy, who had performed a similar chore for Gibbons in St. Louis. McCarthy has since left the union and the department now is supervised by James Harding, a general organizer who once had edited the *Oregon Teamster*. The actual department chores are handled by James Portwine, a Washington publicist, Allen Biggs, former editor of the *Rocky Mountain Teamster,* and H. J. Hicks, former editor of the *Colorado Labor Advocate*. In addition to fielding queries from newspapermen, the department prepares a fortnightly news service for some fifty regional or local union papers. Hoffa does not rely upon the department personnel, whom he considers technicians, for advice on public relations. When he does listen to others, he usually depends on Gibbons, Bufalino, or Zagri for counsel.

The *International Teamster,* the union's monthly magazine, has an average monthly circulation of 1,312,000 and an estimated readership of 3,510,000 and boasts that it is "the largest labor publication in the world." Although it has a formal subscription rate of $2.50 a year, almost the entire issue is distributed free to union members whose names are submitted by the locals. (It is worth noting that the International apparently lacks the names and addresses of some 400,000 members because some locals are willing to pay dues but not submit membership lists.) The cost of publication and distribution during 1960 was $960,341, or 13 per cent of the annual dues income. It is a lively, illustrated magazine, usually 32 pages in size, which contains not only union news but some technical information on trucking, a reminiscent column of events a half-century ago and—an absolute must in modern labor journalism—its quota of jokes. The actual editing is done by Portwine and Biggs, with occasional help from Harding, and as a rule neither Hoffa nor Gibbons sees the contents until page proofs are ready. There have been occasional deletions of articles for policy or strategic reasons but the proofs usually are approved without comment.[12] The magazine was the subject of a bitter comment in 1958 by Godfrey Schmidt, one of the monitors, who complained of "the blatant manner in which the union avenues of communication have been used consistently and almost exclusively for the purpose of self-glorification and propaganda." [13] Although this is partially true (as it is in all house organs), the magazine also has reported at length on topics divorced from internal union problems, and most of the information in it, although presented from the administration's point of view, is factual and well-written. The magazine naturally has reflected Hoffa's strategy and tactics. During the union's futile attempt to prevent passage of the Landrum-Griffin bill, it carried numerous articles attacking the proposed legislation and devoted an entire issue to "the real story" after the bill was passed. Similarly, when Hoffa finally broke with the Board of Monitors and decided on a policy of noncooperation, the magazine again spearheaded the fight, publishing an oversize issue which quoted at length from court documents filed by the union's lawyers.[14]

Teamsters legislative lobbyists usually have been aligned with trucking industry spokesmen in seeking protective legislation or fighting off discriminatory proposals. Recently, the union initiated a national campaign to amend the Interstate Commerce Act in an effort to force the Interstate Commerce Commission to consider the effect on trucking competition of rate-cutting by the railroads in hauling autos and piggy-back cargoes. Sidney Zagri, the union's legislative spokesman, joined industry leaders in opposing administration proposals to increase truck taxes for highway purposes. Again, the Teamsters joined with other transport unions and private railroad and trucking industry spokesmen in protesting "post office competition"—a proposal to allow the post office to carry larger and heavier parcel post. Interestingly enough, despite the usual rivalry between the Teamsters and the railroad unions, Hoffa looked with favor upon attempts by rail unionists to block railroad mergers—a point of view which probably arose from the Teamsters' pro-truck orientation.[15] But the union's most intensive lobbying campaign—and its most abject failure—was its attempt in 1959 to block passage of the Landrum-Griffin law.

The decision to conduct a full-scale lobbying campaign against the law was made early in 1959 despite a widespread pessimism that such a campaign could be successful. Aside from their appearances alongside industry spokesmen, Teamster officials had little experience in the congressional lobbies and, in the past, had relied on the AFL or AFL-CIO for such chores. Even the Hobbs law of 1946, which was aimed directly at Teamsters practices, did not spur the union to intensive legislative activity. But the AFL-CIO's refusal to oppose the 1958 Kennedy-Ives labor reform bill forced upon Hoffa the realization that the Teamsters would stand alone in 1959. Zagri, a lawyer who had directed a local political program for Gibbons in St. Louis, was transferred to Washington to handle the campaign. He developed the strategy of inviting senators and representatives to breakfast with joint council leaders from their home states. The invitation was extended by the joint council (although the International picked up the tab), and few congressmen were ready to snub a bid from the "grass roots." At the breakfast, Zagri and David Previant, the union's labor counsel, usually let loose with a blistering attack on the proposed law, charging that it gave the Secretary of Labor virtually unlimited discretionary powers and junked traditional union procedures. The Teamsters' lobbying tactics became a subject of controversy, and some congressmen complained that they had been threatened and bullied. Although some gains were made in committee amendments, especially in establishing "due process"—notice of hearing, proper procedures, and the right of appeal—as a curb on the secretary's extensive powers, the final bill, as passed by Congress, was described by Previant as "infinitely worse" than that proposed by the committee.[16]

But the futile campaign had an electric effect on Hoffa and other leaders. During its course, Hoffa had gone on a barnstorming, cross-country tour to rouse the local unions to the bill's dangers. His meetings were attended not only by Teamsters members but in many cases by officials of AFL-CIO local unions who were disturbed by the AFL-CIO's refusal to oppose the legislation aggressively. His reception, especially by rank-and-file Teamsters members, convinced Hoffa that the union was ready for a concerted campaign for political action—something that Gibbons had been preaching for years. Hoffa's participation in politics before this had been limited to contacts with individual officeholders and politicians. He considered himself a political independent, supported both Republican and Democratic candidates on different occasions, and in 1956 had voted for President Eisenhower's election. But stung by the legislative defeat in Congress and heartened by the apparent willingness of joint council leaders to accept national leadership on political action, he put the union squarely into the political arena. "We have no choice but to fight," he asserted. At its next meeting, the general executive board followed his lead and authorized establishment of a department of legislation and political education "for the first time in the union's history." [17]

The Teamsters had been active in politics before but never on the scale Hoffa proposed. Dan Tobin, a loyal Democrat, served four years as labor chairman of the Democratic party during the New Deal years and, before the Taft-Hartley act outlawed the practice, contributed sizable donations to Democratic coffers from the union treasury. In 1944, the board called a "national meeting" of local union officials in Washington at which President Roosevelt kicked off his campaign for an unprecedented fourth term. But the union's political role, limited to hortatory pleadings, ignored vote-gathering in the precincts. Under Beck, even this element was absent. Beck, a staunch Republican, was unable to prevent the 1952 convention from giving a rousing endorsement to the Democratic candidate, Adlai E. Stevenson, but the resolution was buried in the convention records. In 1956, the board took no formal action on either presidential candidate, and the union's magazine reflected an apathetic neutrality.

At the local level, of course, many joint councils and local unions always had been active in political work. One of the most far-reaching programs was that of the California joint councils, organized into the California Teamsters Legislative Council, which employed a full-time legislative lobbyist. A number of prominent Teamsters have been elected to national and state office. Two California congressmen, John Shelley and Jeffrey Cohelan, are former union officers, and other Teamsters, often business agents, sit in various state legislatures. At these levels, some Teamsters sided with the Republicans as others did with the Democrats. For a while, Minneapolis Teamsters were closely aligned with the "young Republican" movement led by Harold Stassen, although they later switched to support of the hybrid Democratic-Farmer-Labor Party. John O'Rourke of New York served as head of the Republican labor committee when Dewey ran for governor, although he too later shifted ground and helped form the independent Brotherhood Party in 1960 with old-line AFL-CIO leaders. In Detroit, where Hoffa frequently supported Republicans, the joint council hewed to a nonpartisan line by hiring two lobbyists, one to work on each side of the political street. But most of these local efforts were backed with money instead of precinct work. "The union, at least in the West," one observer noted, "makes little or no effort to deliver the vote of its members. What the union does deliver is money." [18]

Dave Beck, who often had grandiose ambitions, in 1940 had formed an organization called the Joint Council Promotional League, organized on a precinct and block basis and intended to mobilize Teamsters strength for community and political campaigns. But the organization was unable to withstand defeat and, after some setbacks at the polls, limited itself to purely social activities.[19] A political organization with greater staying power was formed by Gibbons' home local in St. Louis. Through a system of monthly neighborhood meetings and an annual city-wide session, the local injected itself in a variety of civic causes from rat control to charter reform. The community steward assembly, as it is called, has not formally engaged in partisan politics but obviously has constructed the foundation and frame for an effective political apparatus.[20] But this was an isolated case and, as Hoffa discovered, he had to build his political organization from the ground up.

As finally approved by the general executive board, the new organization was called DRIVE (Democratic-Republican-Independent Voter Education) with a national committee composed of the union's board and an administrative committee of Hoffa, Gibbons, and Zagri as executive director.[21] It outlined its administrative goals in a five-part Action Series in Practical Precinct Politics, published by the union's political education department. These followed closely Gibbons' concept of a community action group, utilizing community stewards (parallel to the union's traditional shop steward organization) for political work at the precinct level.

If a union member cannot be persuaded to vote for the union's choice, it suggested, forget about him but concentrate on getting the more compliant member to the polls. DRIVE also distributed a series of documentary films, including an attack on the Landrum-Griffin law and the union's version of the Senate committee hearings.

Hoffa's initial proposal to finance the union's political campaign (since union funds legally could not be used to support candidates for federal office) was to apply an ingenious method which Gibbons had developed in St. Louis— voluntary signature cards by which Teamsters members would authorize spending a portion of dues money for political purposes. But Hoffa backed off when Gibbons, Zagri, and other local officials were indicted for violating the federal ban on political contributions. Although the St. Louis leaders later were acquitted of the charge, Hoffa never revived the plan. Instead, he first announced that the financing of the program would be left to decisions of each joint council, then later decided on $3 annual membership dues. Such funds, of course, are intended for use as political contributions and direct support of candidates. The expense for DRIVE itself, limited to voter education and registration and get-out-the-vote campaigns, is borne by the International Union. The union's annual expense statement for 1960 did not isolate funds spent by the legislative and political education department, but the total for department and divisional expenses was $180,000 more than in 1958. A union source was quoted during the campaign as asserting that DRIVE had contributed a million dollars to various candidates.[22]

DRIVE's election strategy in 1960 was relatively simple— to seek to defeat John F. Kennedy for president and to concentrate on 106 congressional districts where congressmen had stood fast against passage of the Landrum-Griffin law or, if they had voted for it, came from the "marginal" districts where elections were won by a 5 per cent majority or less. In the presidential race the general executive board made no official endorsement, but Hoffa made clear his feelings about Kennedy. "I simply cannot see how he can be supported by any trade unionist," he declared. There had been newspaper reports as early as December 1959 that Oakley Hunter, a former California congressman, had asked Hoffa for Teamsters support for Nixon, but the Teamsters approach was to assail Kennedy rather than praise Nixon. During the campaign, Hoffa charged that Kennedy was "unworthy of the trust to be President" and Zagri barnstormed the country, warning that "a Kennedy victory will have a direct effect upon our collective bargaining contracts." Two weeks before the election, the Teamsters News Service devoted more than half of its material to anti-Kennedy propaganda and included as a suggested article a favorable report on Nixon's stand against communist aggression.

The union leadership faced a delicate problem in its opposition to Kennedy since most of the joint councils and local unions were committed to Democratic candidates for lesser office. In one issue, the union magazine used pictures to show union members how to split a ballot as an aid to "those who wish to withhold their vote from Kennedy but who wish to vote for other Democratic candidates." The Teamsters made no effort to take credit for the thinness of the Kennedy victory, but a Teamster newspaper remarked, as "an interesting footnote," that Kennedy had won only four of the 13 states in the Central States area and had lost the popular vote in the area by a million ballots.[23]

DRIVE also did poorly in the congressional races. It was active in 233 congressional races and its candidate won in 137, but many of these districts were "safe" for the incumbent. In the more crucial marginal districts, the record showed fewer victories. DRIVE had concentrated its efforts in 39 of the 56 marginal districts whose representatives had voted for Landrum-Griffin, but defeated only one of them. On the other hand, it made a major effort to return some 50 congressmen who had opposed Landrum-Griffin, but lost in eight cases. DRIVE, incidentally, supported Democrats in 204 cases, Republicans in 28 others, and one Liberal.[24]

DRIVE's failure in the 1960 elections did not dishearten Hoffa, and the department continued to function at a fast pace. Before the 1961 convention, Hoffa called a special political session of all delegates and urged the union's business agents to pay as much attention to politics as to bargaining and grievances. "It's not the picket line or organizing," he declared, "but politics which will determine where we'll be five years from now." The convention itself passed a resolution proposing that, "wherever practicable," each joint council engage a full-time political director, but it did not take the next step of writing this into the constitution. Immediately after the convention, DRIVE concentrated on the formation of women's auxiliaries, apparently in the belief that it would be easier to activate wives than members. But the union still faces an uphill pull in its political efforts. Some joint council leaders are fearful that a successful national political organization will counter their own political activity at the local level while others are merely apathetic. Nor are some political leaders enthusiastic about the formation of a separate Teamsters political grouping. Apprehensive that open Teamsters endorsement may well result in defeat for the union's choice, some of them would prefer to have the Teamsters quietly support more acceptable labor political organizations.[25]

All told, the magnificent Teamsters headquarters building in Washington houses less than 100 persons, including some 17 maintenance personnel. (The 1961 convention authorized the moving of the union's "principal and main office" to Detroit but this was a legal maneuver, designed to ease the union's many courtroom problems, and the operating headquarters has remained in Washington.)[26] Working conditions for some 50 clerical employes (none of whom is a union member) are nearly ideal. The workweek is 35 hours, and compensation is fixed at levels paralleling those of the federal government, the area's largest employer. Employes of the International Union are eligible for a generous retirement plan which provides benefits to an employe retiring at the age of 62 after 15 years' service. First established in 1951, the employer-paid plan costs the union some $425,000 a year. English, who serves as its trustee, reported to the 1961 convention that it has a net worth of $5,207,942, almost all of which was invested in federal securities.[27]

The headquarters building itself is worthy of mention. An air-conditioned, $5,000,000 structure overlooking the capital, it was built by Beck in 1955 in his drive toward respectability. It is a sumptuous palace, with a marble-finished 100-foot lobby, a 474-seat auditorium, luxurious offices, spacious conference rooms, and paneled lounges. Almost all its furnishings are described in superlatives. The lectern in the auditorium, according to a brochure distributed at the dedication, is duplicated only by another in the White House; the directors' table in the general executive board conference room is "one of the two largest in the United States." In 1960, use of the building cost some $410,620, including $58,303 in taxes and $97,774 in depreciation. It is more in keeping with Beck's conception of the union's grandeur than with Hoffa's, but it cannot easily be sold nor can its excess space be let to other tenants. With its marble-finished corridors and columns faced with imported Venetian mosaic, it serves as an expensive "white elephant" to remind the current tenants that there once was a man named Beck.

6

The Conference

The relationship between the Teamsters International Union and its locals, once marked by a simple exchange of dues for a charter, has become a complex, interlaced network of intermediary organizations. Because the pace of change has been irregular through the years, the union's power structure often defies clear delineation. But it is evident that the rise of the area conference marks the end of the local union as a significant factor in collective bargaining. And even as the area conference reaches maturity, it is pursued by the shadow of the next step toward a truly national union—the national union trade division and industry council. Meanwhile, the joint council, which some local leaders once hoped would become a base for union power, plays a diminished role in the bargaining structure and its future lies in the arena of political action.

The area conference has not yet completely replaced the local union in the bargaining function but it is rapidly doing so. The conference is in itself a smaller replica of the

International Union, self-contained administratively with its own organization staffs, comprised of all locals within its geographic boundaries. By constitutional mandate, it is an "organic body" of the International Union, financed equally by the International and its affiliated locals. Its potential danger as a union within a union is so evident that the constitution insists that conference activities "shall, at all times, be subject to the unqualified direction and control of the general president." The president names the conference director, usually a vice-president, and must approve the conference bylaws. In any case, he may make any amendments or changes in the bylaws, even after approval, "as he deems to be in the best interest of the International Union." [1]

The conference concept is barely a quarter-century old, and it was not integrated into the union's administrative structure until 1947. In the thirties, when it was developed, it was intended to play an organization rather than a bargaining role. The idea originated on the west coast in 1934 and was taken over in 1937 by Minneapolis Local 544, then led by a group of Trotzkyist Communists. Farrell Dobbs, a Local 544 organizer assigned to over-the-road operations, recognized that highway drivers, because of their strategic position in regulating the flow of intercity freight, were all potential organizers and their refusal to service a nonunion freight depot could compel the organization of the local cartage drivers and dock freight handlers. Hoffa later expanded the concept to take in specialized trucking as well. "Without the city cartage and the road organized in a territory," he said, "you cannot organize the rest of the city. Any employer who wants to fight you in any other branch of our business can whip the strongest local union unless you have the support of the road and city cartage. But once you organize the road, the city, the warehouses, nobody can whip the Teamsters union, nobody." [2] Tobin did not welcome the new movement with enthusiasm but finally allowed locals from five midwestern cities to meet together in June 1938 and effect "a working agreement for collaboration." Two months later, the first area agreement in the union's history was signed, covering eleven states. A parallel development along the Pacific coast soon brought in its wake demands that the International grant the new structure sufficient authority to prevent small local unions from settling contracts below area standards. The 1947 convention, at Beck's urging, finally took a half-hearted step in this direction by giving the general board power to order the affiliation of local unions with a conference if a majority of locals within the conference jurisdiction already had joined. By 1961, the constitution provided that all local unions and joint councils "must affiliate with and participate in" conference activities, paying a minimum of five cents a month per member to the conference.

The 1961 convention also strengthened the conference role in bargaining. If a majority of affiliated locals vote for area negotiations, all locals must participate in such bargaining and are bound by the resulting contract. Such a contract, if approved by "a majority of the votes cast by local union members," is a binding document and a protesting local may not withdraw from it. (There is a significant difference of wording between the majority necessary to open negotiations and that necessary to ratify a contract. In the first case, it is a majority of locals, giving smaller locals power to force a reluctant large local into line. In the second, it is a majority of members, preventing smaller locals from vetoing contract ratification.) Some delegates to the 1957 convention, where the mandatory contract was first accepted, protested that it could wipe out existing bargaining patterns. James T. Lukens of Cincinnati, who four years later bolted the union, pointed out that a chain might cover only a fraction of local members in any one city yet set the city wage pattern, since locals often provide the same contract for all competitive employers. Other delegates argued that it would force locals with higher-than-area working conditions "to sit by the wayside while other (locals) are brought up to par." [3]

The objectors were correct in their forebodings. The

concept of a mandatory conference and a binding contract was intended to wipe out the prized autonomy of local unions to settle on working conditions either above or below the area level. The 1961 convention gave an objecting local a possible way out by allowing it to appeal to the general executive board if it believed the contract would deprive its members of "better existing conditions," but only the board can decide "whether such alleged better general conditions shall be continued or shall yield to the overall gains of the proposed contract." Meanwhile, local autonomy in area bargaining enjoyed its last fling in the fall of 1961 when local cartage drivers in the San Francisco area, with hourly rates up to 34 cents an hour higher than elsewhere in the west, rejected a 20-cent raise over three years proposed by Hoffa, and finally accepted a 28-cent hike. Hoffa then negotiated an 11-state pact with 45 cents in higher wages for the three years, making up the remaining 17 cents by 1965.[4]

The multi-state area pacts obviously are but a step toward Hoffa's ultimate goal—a national pact with uniform nationwide conditions. Hoffa's advocacy of common expiration dates for all area pacts in any one industry became more urgent after the Landrum-Griffin law outlawed the Teamsters' "hot cargo" clause through which the union enforced sanctions against a nonunion employer or a firm on strike. The union rewrote the clause to provide for triple-pay penalty in case its members were compelled to cross picket lines, but the National Labor Relations Board immediately challenged the new clause and the issue is now being litigated. Hoffa has long been an advocate of area agreements, which he has described as "major pillars in the (union's) collective bargaining structure." [5] His proposal for a national master freight agreement, however, aroused a furious storm with its implication of a potential national truck strike. Hoffa has steadfastly denied that the union plans to enforce its contract demands through a national shutdown. "At no time, and I make this as a flat statement," he asserted, "will there ever be a nationwide strike of over-the-road, (local) cartage and dock. It just isn't good business for the union." [6] His repeated assurances failed to still the clamor, but he nevertheless went ahead with his program for common expiration dates and succeeded in winning his way in a number of industries, including highway freight transport.

The area agreements, by and large, are the source of the huge pension trusts which, Hoffa estimated late in 1961, have amassed some $600 million in reserves and are growing at a rapid pace.[7] These pension funds should be distinguished from the health and welfare (hospitalization and sick benefit) funds which the Senate committee charged were milked by excessive commissions.[8] The pension funds generally are financed by employer payments in accord with union contract provisions and pile up huge reserves with which to pay future pensions. The largest of these is the Central States, Southeast, and Southwest Area Fund, which has $150 million in reserves and is growing by $30 million a year.[9] It is administered by a committee of seven employer and seven union representatives, including Hoffa and Gordon Conklin of St. Paul, a Teamsters vice-president. Actual day-to-day administration is directed by Francis Murtha, a general organizer who has remained on the union's payroll and thus is subject to Hoffa's orders. Despite the theoretical bipartisan control, there is general agreement that the crucial power of deciding where the fund's reserves will be invested rests with Hoffa, subject to recommendations from the fund's financial consultants. The inference that Hoffa makes the final decision was bolstered by a Senate committee probe of a proposed $300,000 loan from the fund to Louis (Babe) Triscaro, a Cleveland Teamsters leader, which was to finance an arms-smuggling venture to Cuba.[10] Occasionally, the fund's investments can place the union in a strange bargaining position. An example of this occurred in 1960 when the United Rubber Workers began an organizing drive among employes of the Auburn Rubber Company, Deming, New Mexico. The company threatened to close the city-financed plant if the Rubber Workers won, jeopardizing some $3,000,-

000 in municipal bonds held by the pension fund. The Teamsters promptly moved in with a rival organizing drive and won representation rights in a National Labor Relations Board election.[11]

There are four area conferences, each with clear geographic outlines. The Western Conference includes 11 western states, Hawaii, Alaska, and three western Canadian conferences. The Central Conference is comprised of the 13 midwestern states and two central Canadian provinces, and the Eastern Conference stretches from the eastern Canadian provinces through the Atlantic states as far south as North and South Carolina. The remaining 9 southern states are assigned to the Southern Conference, except for an area around El Paso, Texas, which is affiliated with the Phoenix joint council for economic reasons. All conferences have similar structures, although they are marked by occasional variations from pattern. In each case, the international director is appointed by the general president and subject to his direction; he shares policy-making authority with a committee elected by delegates at annual or biennial meetings. Dues income includes the 5-cent monthly payment per member from the international union and at least that much from affiliated locals. Vice-presidents from the area sit on the policy committee, serving as another safeguard that the conference will adhere to the strategic line laid down by the International Union. Representation at the meetings is based on the unit principle, rather than the proportionate size of the affiliate, thus giving smaller locals and councils considerable veto power. The conference session is "in no sense a convention," Frank Brewster, then Western Conference chairman, explained in 1957, "it is rather a business meeting of the business representatives employed by the participating local unions." [12] This concept is enforced in the Central and Eastern conferences by limiting delegates to "employed officers or business agents" of affiliates and, in the Central Conference, the local's business agent automatically is a delegate.

The Western Conference of Teamsters is the oldest and best-developed of the conferences. It includes some 260 local unions in 11 joint councils with a total average membership of 361,000 (although actual membership may range as high as 375,000 at the peak of the canning season). Some 63 per cent of its membership is concentrated in California, and another 23 per cent is located in Oregon and Washington. It has 13 trade divisions, 7 of which have full-time directors, and it also operates full scale research, public relations, and legal departments. Einar Mohn, who has headed the conference under Hoffa, has been a union vice-president since 1952 and served as Beck's administrative assistant. Before 1961, the conference per capita dues were 62 cents a member, of which 15 cents was allocated for general expenses, 5 cents to organizing, 17 cents to a retirement fund for some 1,300 officers and employes of affiliated locals and joint councils, and 25 cents to a strike benefit fund. The 1961 meeting voted to eliminate the 25-cent strike benefit payment, in view of the decision by the International to raise strike benefits, but directed that the $2,500,000 fund on hand continue to be spent until exhausted. The principal business of the conference is not conducted in its general meetings but in periodic trade division meetings where union leaders with common problems meet to exchange ideas and information and plan strategy for pending negotiations.[13]

The Central Conference, Hoffa's personal domain, is the youngest of the area groups and second-largest. As of April 1, 1961, it had a membership of 442,201 in 295 local unions, with almost 70 per cent of its members concentrated in the states of Illinois, Ohio, Missouri, and Michigan. Unlike the other conferences, it has never had a full-time directing official. Hoffa, who was its first chairman (and has continued as director while he has been general president), also served as supervising vice-president for the Eastern and Southern Conferences before 1957. Since then, John T. O'Brien of Chicago has been acting chairman, but his primary responsibility has always been his home local. However, both Hoffa and Gibbons, the conference secretary-treasurer, keep in constant touch with midwestern affairs. The conference is financed by the minimum 10 cents per member, divided between the international and local unions. This apparently is more than adequate; the financial report for fiscal 1960-1961 showed a surplus of $134,871, despite organizing expense of $362,927. One of the conference's most fruitful functions is performed by its research department which produces, in conjunction with the chairman's report, penetrating economic analyses of various aspects of the union's widespread jurisdiction.[14]

The Eastern Conference, like the Central Conference, was organized under Beck, who was anxious to weld the eastern locals into a cohesive weapon because he had given up hope of organizing the South through normal recruiting campaigns. "If the eastern states would form an organization similar to the western," he urged in 1945, "we could all cooperate in a unified move to organize the South. We then would be in a position to shut off the South completely from boat, rail, and truck merchandise with the rest of the country. We can't organize the South in the South, but it will be a different story if the South can't move its crops or import supplies." [15] The Eastern Conference is headed by Thomas E. Flynn, a union vice-president who served as Tobin's executive assistant from 1941 to 1952. As of March, 1962, it had a total membership of 559,670 in 18 joint councils, with more than half concentrated in New York City, eastern Pennsylvania, and northern New Jersey. For many years, the eastern locals—the oldest in the international and most possessive of their autonomy—resisted attempts to coordinate their bargaining efforts, but this resistance has lessened under the impact of Hoffa's insistence upon area contracts. Hoffa reported to the 1961 convention that the number of freight contracts within the Eastern Conference has declined from 120 to less than 20. Conference research department surveys in 1954 and 1955 disclosed that many industries in the East, traditionally regarded as union strongholds, still were largely unorganized, especially in smaller cities. The reports disclosed that 40 per cent of 5,700 employes of the four largest moving companies were nonunion; so were 25 per cent of 31,300 bakery drivers and 40 per cent of 77,000 dairy employes.[16]

The Southern Conference, although organized in 1942, is the smallest and weakest of the four area groups. It includes 48 locals in 8 joint councils with some 90,000 members. Thirty-six of these locals were entitled to only one delegate at the 1961 convention, indicating a membership of less than 1,000, and only Atlanta could boast of a local with more than 5,000 members. The conference is directed by Murray W. Miller, a vice-president who has been a general organizer since 1946. Miller directs an organizing staff of six, including Ralph Dixon, conference secretary-treasurer, who also is a general organizer. Except for warehousing, its five active trade divisions are skeleton organizations.[17]

Canadian locals were united in the Canadian Conference of Teamsters until June, 1961, but they now are affiliated to the three principal area conferences. Some 44 locals from Canada were on the 1961 delegate roster, all but 11 with a single delegate. There are five joint councils, but only Toronto and Vancouver embrace a sizable membership. The union's total Canadian membership in 1962 was 40,000. Some of the Canadian Teamsters have been seeking a separate Canadian organization, and local union delegates voted in 1960 to establish a Canadian coordinating committee, financed by a 1-cent monthly per capita tax.[18] The principal figure in the Canadian organization is L. M. "Casey" Dodds of Windsor, Ontario, a general organizer, who also serves as Central Conference director in Canada.

The core of the area conference rests in the trade divisions, industry-wide groups which meet periodically to exchange information and discuss strategy in forthcoming negotiations. The constitutional directive for mandatory area bargaining, even without the consent of local unions, emphasizes the role these groups play in the collective bargaining process. The various area trade divisions are expected to become the nuclei of national industry groups, especially as the union is faced with the problems presented by national corporations with a unified labor policy. There have been national trade divisions for many years, especially in the bakery and dairy industries, but their general development still is in the formative stage. Some sixteen national trade divisions have been formed, generally paralleling the industry lines of the area conference groups. But only five divisions have full-time directors, and the others are led by local union leaders who must necessarily subordinate national issues to immediate problems. Few of the divisions have even fulfilled the minimum task set for them by Gibbons in 1953: "We will be a small national staff, a kind of planning board, which will gather the facts back to the (area) trade divisions, to the joint councils, and to the local union, and these will at the local level attempt to implement a program which will bring about uniformity of conditions." [19]

Like the area conference when it was first organized, the present emphasis in the national trade division is on organization rather than bargaining. It is noteworthy that the bakery and dairy national divisions, composed of the sales trades (so called because drivers also serve as salesmen and are paid on a commission basis) do not have full-time directors; a third division in the sales trades, the laundry division, recently was dissolved. This indicates the diminishing importance of the sales drivers, who historically constituted the core of the union and supplied most of the policy-making leadership.[20] The decline can be attributed in part to the steadily decreasing use of home deliveries with consequent abolition of retail routes. But it is also caused by the growth of chain-store distribution, especially where large grocery chains establish "captive" bakeries or dairies, usually wholly owned subsidiaries, and then deliver through the use of "drop shipments" without using competitive sales drivers. The general executive board has tried to mediate disputes between the sales locals and the general locals whose members are hourly rated rather than commission salesmen, as the sales locals have protested the invasion of their historical jurisdiction. But the problem is solving itself through the gradual decline of sales locals, especially in the bakery industry.

A recent addition to the list of national trade divisions is the national airlines division, formed after the Teamsters conducted a successful raid in Western Airlines, where the Machinists had represented mechanics and ground personnel. The union, which already represented Pan American employes, joined the two groups into a trade division and announced an aggressive campaign among the 160,000 airline employes—most of whom were members of other unions. The new division met with some immediate organizational setbacks—it lost an election to the Machinists among 1,200 National Airline employes and failed to secure a poll among Trans World Airline workers. Hoffa also offered haven to the airline stewardess group, then involved in an internal dispute with its parent pilots union, but the dissidents chose instead to join the Transport Workers union.[21]

Another area of new organization, this one among a previously unorganized group, is agriculture. The union has represented closely allied cannery packing and processing workers for more than two decades, and recently scored what it described as a major breakthrough among field workers when it signed a contract with a large California grower. The union also has been active among poultry and dairy farmers in the East, concentrating upon organization of small, independent farmers rather than hired hands. It also has stressed organization campaigns among industrial workers where the union now claims some 250,000 members. A plum apparently ripe for picking is the presence of thousands of unorganized clerical employes in the offices of trucking firms. Some 3,500 already have been brought into the union in the Chicago area, and campaigns to expand this sector have been under way in the East and West.[22]

The 1961 convention paved the way for union growth

through merger with other organizations by giving the general executive board "full power and exclusive authority" to negotiate the "absorption, amalgamation, merger, or affiliation of or coordination with other labor organizations." This wide sweep of authority was soon put into effect when the board agreed to accept the affiliation of the Laundry Workers Union.[23]

The joint council is the final subordinate level in the International Union structure, except for the local union itself. As we have seen, the onrush of area bargaining has reduced the council's power in the economic sector, but it nevertheless remains as a vital channel of communication between the International and the local union. The joint council concept is as old as the union itself and was incorporated in the constitution in 1904. It theoretically covers a metropolitan area but can, and often does, extend state wide or even spill over state boundaries. In 1961, only eight states had two or more councils and efforts have continued to merge these groups into single state-wide councils, albeit hampered by existing personal rivalries among incumbent officers. Representation in the council is based upon the unit, with each local union entitled to a delegation composed of its seven-man executive board. Few of the council officers serve as full-time paid functionaries, although all the councils employ permanent staffs of organizers and clerical help. However, the council's officers usually are regarded as the union's spokesmen in the community and the community's spokesmen within the International. In addition to functioning as a channel of communication between the locals and higher bodies, especially on bargaining problems involving contracts and strikes, the council also serves as a primary arbiter of jurisdictional conflicts between its affiliated locals and as a subordinate court of appeals in the union's judicial machinery.

The joint councils range in size from giant organizations like New York City with more than 160,000 members, Chicago with 146,000, and Los Angeles with 105,000, to tiny

Auburndale, Florida, with 400, and Winnipeg with 1,200.[24] Under a 1961 constitutional amendment, the council was given delegate representation to the international convention and has always enjoyed similar prerogatives at area conferences. Shortly after Hoffa assumed office, he proposed to bring joint council leaders together periodically to issue statements of national policy but apparently abandoned the idea after trying it twice.[25] But with the current emphasis on political action, it is evident that the joint councils are being prepared to assume a new and important role within the union.

7

The Local Union

At the base of the pyramid of the International Union are some 900 local unions and their 1,700,000 members. Despite the intervention of joint councils and area and trade conferences between the local union and the parent body, there remains a direct bond between top and bottom, reinforced by constitutional directives and actual practice. Locals come in all sizes and shapes and may have little in common except their Teamsters affiliation. Their governmental practices often are a reflection of local-level leadership goals, prodded or ignored by an interested or apathetic rank and file. Some locals, like Gibbons' Local 688 in St. Louis, have become outstanding showpieces of internal democracy, evolving an elaborate system of responsible parliamentary government, while others are content with token membership meetings and the unlimited authority to top officers. The charter contract between the International and the local union stresses that whatever rights and privileges the local union enjoys come as a grant from the International and are subject to revocation. Other sections of the constitution make it equally clear that the extent of self-government granted the local depends wholly upon the discretion of the International, subject to internal judicial appeals. In practice, of course, such discretion is exercised with many variations and, as we shall see, at one time 109 locals were under trusteeship, that is, deprived of the right of self-government. It is not necessarily true that any intervention by an international into local affairs is evil or that the unrestricted exercise of local government is good per se. Indeed, one of the instructions of the federal court which established the Board of Monitors mandated the drafting of "a model code of local union by-laws," with its clear implication that many local union memberships were incapable of insuring proper self-government.

The first of the International's powers is the exercise of its discretion whether to grant the charter. For many years in the union's history, charters were a kind of patronage to be dispensed by vice-presidents to favorites seeking a facade of authority, as well as the legitimate grant of a local union to a group of workers. In Minneapolis, for instance, Sidney L. Brennan was instrumental in 1952 in securing a charter for Gerald P. Connelly, although Connelly had neither members nor jurisdiction.[1] The scandals attending the chartering of the New York "paper locals" (in a move by Hoffa to control the New York joint council) forced extensive changes in this process by the 1957 convention. Under present regulations, the charter applications must be signed by seven prospective members, subject to review but not veto by the affected joint council, and approved by the general president, secretary-treasurer and the general executive board. Charters usually define a limited industrial and territorial jurisdiction, although the 1961 constitution allows unlimited geographical grants, "upon such terms and under such conditions as the general executive board shall consider appropriate." [2]

Locals come and go. Some locals, the by-products of ambitious but abortive organization campaigns, have a short life, like Local 275 for Great Lakes seamen, chartered and dissolved in the same convention period. A revoked charter can be granted to an organization far removed from its former possessor; Local 10, for instance, was originally a general drivers' local in Juneau, Alaska, but its charter later was granted to a local with unlimited jurisdiction in the state of Nebraska, then transformed into a public employes' charter, and finally dissolved.[3] The original intention of the union's founders was to restrict each local to a single craft jurisdiction, and the constitution theoretically allows formation of a mixed local only "whenever there is not a sufficient number of any one craft." In practice, mixed locals have become the rule for newly chartered affiliates except when already organized groups, like the brewery locals, come into the Teamsters as a unit.

Under constitutional mandate, the locals are required to accept any applicant for membership unless he is a member or follower of the Communist Party or has "willfully" refused to become a citizen of the United States or Canada.[4] Before the 1961 convention, the applicants were required to be "of good moral character" and to have declared their intention of attaining citizenship. Like many other constitutional changes, these phrases were altered or deleted in a legal maneuver to avert possible court challenges of the eligibility of some union leaders to membership. This also explains why the 1961 convention dropped a prohibition against admitting members of any "other subversive organization," except the Communist Party. Hoffa explained that he feared that the union's enemies might use the House Un-American Activities Committee's "wild accusations to raise some subversive question against every man sitting here."[5] The power to ban Communists is a wide one and expressly gives the general president authority to review a "not guilty" finding by the local union trial board if, in his opinion, "the section has not been complied with in principle or intent." The anti-Communist clause was inserted in 1935 when Minneapolis Local 574 was led by Trotskyist Communists, and its enforcement, like that of other sections of the constitution, often varies with the times. In 1953, Beck induced 10 locals of the Brewery Workers Union to bolt to the Teamsters and apparently was not deterred by the fact that three of the rebel leaders had refused to testify on possible Communist affiliations while under congressional investigation. Again in 1956, former officers of a United Public Workers local, ousted from the CIO for pro-Communist leadership, showed up as business agents for a Teamsters public employe local in New York.[6]

Despite the eligibility of "any person" for union membership, in practice locals have been given wide authority to limit their membership in accord with work requirements. Owner-operators cannot be denied membership unless the general president agrees that their membership would be detrimental to the local's welfare, but contracts covering the use of their labor and equipment cannot be used to reduce the wage scale. Nor can a local union refuse to accept on transfer a member of a sister local if he is working within its jurisdiction. On the other hand, members leaving the union's jurisdiction (either by moving out of the geographic limits or working at another craft or occupation) can no longer remain members and must be given honorable withdrawal cards, but retired workers, if the union agrees, may continue as honorary members and remain eligible for life insurance and sick benefits. Members holding jobs in other jurisdictions continue paying dues to the first organization but must pay a periodic service fee (not in excess of normal dues) to the second.[7]

Another internal problem affecting the eligibility of individual members arises out of racketeering. Racketeering has been defined as "the use of union office or power for personal profit," manifesting itself in such acts as bribery, embezzlement, "sweetheart" contracts, payoffs to prevent organization or avert strikes, collusion to establish monopolies "which are in the interest of employers, material dealers, and union officers," and kickbacks and rebates on health and welfare contracts.[8] To this list might be added conflicts of interest which discourage effective unionism, manipulation of union funds for personal gain, and denial of internal democracy to prevent disclosure of financial malfeasance. Racketeering is not a new thing in the labor movement and has been a problem within the Teamsters throughout the union's history. The Senate committee hearings concentrated on the Teamsters Union and devoted 34 of its 58 volumes to the Teamsters, its officers and locals.[9] The index to some 46,150 pages of testimony from 1,526 witnesses lists 183 Teamsters locals, including some 40 in which the committee uncovered indications of bribery, payoffs, extortion, and other evidences of racketeering. These included issuance of charters to locals controlled by crooks and hoodlums, creation of "juke-box" locals which served as an industry "whip" to coerce noncooperative employers into line, use of locals to enforce extortion practices by employer "associations," wholesale looting of union treasuries, and use of union positions for personal aggrandizement. One observer summed up the committee's accusations by citing "volumes of uncontroverted evidence that the union is crawling with extortionists, racketeers, and sweetheart contractors." [10]

One difficulty in discussing labor racketeering is that it often is difficult to distinguish between actions intended for personal gain and similar actions which may be illegal by statute but which seek only to improve the welfare of the union and its members. The racketeer's stock in trade is essentially the abuse of practices used by legitimate unions for legitimate ends—tactics like organizational picketing, recognition agreements without worker consent, collusion with employers for price fixing and restraint of trade, and violence during disputes. "Unions may occasionally seek objectives or utilize methods," an observer noted, "which are not approved by many members of the community. Yet such conduct does not indicate venality or corruption, even though it might not be socially desirable." [11]

It is true that some of the committee's allegations failed

of proof in instances where indictments were later brought
before juries, and the record of convictions, upheld on appeal, has been not studded with success. It is also true that
the committee, like other congressional committees before
it, conducted a one-sided inquiry and often was more interested in headlines than perspective. Its most serious charge
was that its amassed evidence of corruption was proof of an
underworld plot to control the nation's largest and most
strategic labor union. Hoffa's rise to power, it warned, "will
place the underworld in a position to dominate American
economic life." But despite its expert staff and three years
of inquiry, the committee was unable to back this belief with
the most elementary proof. Nevertheless, Hoffa's reluctance
to accept any of the committee's charges as worthy of serious
investigation was essentially an evasion of responsibility, and
his decision that intra-union action must await the final
appeal to the highest courts did not serve to curb racketeers
or rid the union of hoodlums. Prodded by the Board of
Monitors, Hoffa did initiate some intra-union investigations
and, in an obvious effort to counter the committee's continuing attack, announced in 1958 the formation of a special
anti-racketeering commission, headed by former Senator
George H. Bender (R., Ohio). Neither was a serious effort.
Indeed, the Bender committee, which cost the union $58,000,
limited itself to receiving self-serving declarations of innocence from accused locals and individuals. Hoffa made it
clear in 1959, in an official union announcement, that "under
no circumstance would he abuse the power of his office to
pacify the political whims of any group inside or outside
the labor movement." [12]

Hoffa certainly had sufficient authority to meet the situation and could have depended upon wide support within
the union and from public opinion if he had done so. He had
the general president's power, if the charges were serious
enough "to jeopardize the interest of the union," to suspend
the accused member pending a decision and, at his discretion, to assume original jurisdiction in such a case. The

constitution, before 1961, specifically gave him authority to revoke the membership of a member convicted of "a crime or serious wrongdoing which tends to bring dishonor upon the union," or who "has engaged in what is commonly termed racketeering." If necessary, he could place the local under trusteeship. As it was, Hoffa not only exercised none of these powers, but urged the convention to delete the clause providing for revocation of the membership of convicted criminals. He noted that the Landrum-Griffin law barred convicted felons only from union office and asked: "Why should this convention go on record and make a more stringent rule?" [13] The convention went even further. It approved a new constitutional section which authorized the general executive board or the local union to pay all legal expenses for an accused officer if it believed the charges he faced were unfounded, politically motivated, or filed in bad faith in an attempt to embarrass or destroy the union, or "if a majority in its sole discretion determines that the expenditure should be made." [14]

The constitution contains only skeleton provisions for the conduct of local unions. It provides that local union membership meetings must take place monthly but that such meetings can be suspended during the summer months. In a paraphrase of the union member's bill of rights, as contained in the Landrum-Griffin law, it guarantees an individual member's right "to express views, arguments, or opinions upon any business properly before the meeting . . . but no member shall evade or avoid his responsibility to the organization as an institution or engage in or instigate any conduct which would interfere with the local union's performance of its legal or contractual obligations." Local unions are allowed to conduct their membership meetings by holding sub-meetings "on a division, craft, place of employment, or other similar basis" and a separate unit is permitted, if it so votes, to charge higher dues, assessments, or initiation fees." [15] Local union bylaws are subject to the approval of the general president and subject to appeal to the general

executive board. They must provide for a seven-man local
executive board, consisting of the president, vice-president,
recording secretary, secretary-treasurer, and three trustees.
Meetings of the local executive board (as well as those of
the general executive board, conference policy committees,
and executive boards of other subordinate bodies) are closed
to rank-and-file members, except by permission.[16]

Local officers are elected for a minimum three-year term
with the maximum at five years, the term of office in the
International Union. A member, with the permission of the
general president, may hold office in two separate locals, even
if he was not a member of the second local before he took
office. Nomination of officers must take place in November or
December, and at least 30 days must elapse between nomination and election. The election must be by secret ballot or
voting machine, and the polling place must be open for at
least six hours. Write-in votes for candidates not nominated
are void. The local executive board is charged with providing "safeguards for the honest and fair conduct" of the
election, including permission for candidates to nominate
any member as an observer. Election is by simple plurality
and, as already noted, election as an officer or business agent
also serves as election as a delegate to the international convention. In case of unopposed nominations, the constitution
provides that no election is necessary. Vacancies among
elected offices during the term of office are filled by appointment of the local executive board.[17]

The general executive board in 1961 recommended to the
locals that they adopt a set of "model local union bylaws,"
as drafted by the Board of Monitors and approved by the
court. However, the recommendation was not mandatory
and Hoffa, in urging locals to consider the proposed bylaws,
stressed that the local was free to retain any section of its
present bylaws which it considered "superior or better
adapted to the local situation." [18] The model bylaws generally include many of the self-government provisions contained in the Landrum-Griffin law. They differ in one sig-

nificant respect from bylaws already used by many locals, for they place the local's principal executive officer (usually the secretary-treasurer) under the firm control of the local executive board and reserve to the board the final authority "to conduct and manage the affairs of this organization." The bylaws also restrict the power of the board to fill vacancies among the officers by requiring that such vacancies, if the unexpired term is for more than two years, must be filled by election.[19]

To be eligible for election to office, a member must be in continuous good standing in his local union for 24 months prior to his nomination and, if the local union so decides, must have attended a minimum number of regular meetings, not to exceed half of those held during this period. The general executive board may waive the requirement that he must have worked in the local union's jurisdiction for at least two years, and incumbents in office during the 1952 convention are protected by a "grandfather" clause from this requirement.[20] The 1961 convention ended a long-standing controversy over the good-standing requirement by providing that good standing be redefined as payment of dues "on or before the last business day of the current month." [21] The previous requirement had been dues payment "on or before the first business day of the current month, in advance" and had made ineligible for office thousands of union members on check off who had become delinquent when their employers had delayed payment until after the first day of the month.

There are two methods by which the International can enforce discipline on a recalcitrant local—revocation or suspension of its charter, or imposition of trusteeship. Revocation or suspension is a method generally used only in cases where the local has become bankrupt and there are no reserves to protect. The more common form of discipline is appointment of a temporary trustee—an act which makes the trustee virtual dictator of the local, allows the membership only such privileges and self-government as the trustee proposes, and generally undertakes a complete reorganization of the local's affairs. Trusteeships, also called receiverships or supervision, are not uncommon in the American labor movement, and they can be used either constructively (where unrestricted self-government might dissipate the local's resources) or destructively (where international officers seek to extend and consolidate their power by suppressing minority opposition). Within the Teamsters, trusteeships have been used both ways. In the usual exercise of a trusteeship, the local union's officers and business agents are appointed instead of elected, but the union's normal routine is not disturbed. Membership meetings continue to be held in normal fashion, the trustee or his appointed officers regularly submit reports of union finances and activities, and the membership continues to vote on many issues, including ratification of contracts or questions of policy—subject, of course, to the reserve veto held by the trustee. On occasion, the membership has overridden the trustee's wishes, as in the 1957 convention when a Pittsburgh local cast its eleven votes for Thomas J. Haggerty of Chicago for president although its trustee, Einar Mohn, was supporting Hoffa. The trustee named by the general president usually is a vice-president or general organizer who may have many other duties, and the union's business is actually conducted by an appointed local officer or a conference or joint council representative.

The power to impose trusteeships was first enacted by the 1908 constitution, when the union faced secessionist uprisings in several areas. Tobin used this power sparingly and only after serious provocation and, in at least one instance, at the request of the local leadership itself. This occurred in 1938 when he placed several New England locals under trusteeship so that members could not blame the local officers for enforcing an unpopular bargaining agreement.[22] The extraordinary powers, already existing in practice, granted to the general president in imposing trusteeships were explicitly written into the constitution in 1940. There was no provision for appeal or review of his decisions or acts, nor was there any limit set on the trusteeship's duration. This unlimited grant of authority was challenged in the civil courts, and the 1952 convention amended the constitution to provide for hearings within 30 days after the trustee's appointment, for appeals to the general executive board and then to the convention from the president's ruling, and for review every six months upon petition from the local union. Unlike Tobin, Beck used the trusteeship weapon freely and, by 1957, 109 locals were under trusteeship.[23] Not all the trusteeships stemmed from the same cause. In St. Louis, where there was some evidence of hoodlum control, Beck put the entire joint council under Thomas E. Flynn as trustee, and Flynn handed over the housekeeping chores to Harold Gibbons. Locals were merged, charters revoked and members transferred, new locals chartered, and four of the five remaining locals were placed under trusteeship. On the other hand, according to the Senate committee, a trusteeship was placed over the Pontiac, Michigan, local after four of the local's officers were convicted of extortion, apparently for the sole purpose of continuing the old regime.[24]

The 1957 convention reinforced the safeguards against unfair trusteeships by providing that, except in emergency situations, hearings must be held before the trusteeship is imposed and within 30 days after the emergency trustee is appointed. The three-man hearing panel must include at least one international vice-president and another "disinterested member" from the affected region. The local union may petition at six-month intervals for restoration of its autonomous rights, and such petitions require new hearings with the usual opportunity for appeal. In any case, the general executive board must undertake a full review of the situation every two years. Most of the 1957 provisions were retained by the 1961 convention, except that the reasons justifying trusteeship were copied from the Landrum-Griffin law and the two-year interval was shortened to 18 months in accordance with legal requirements.[25] Meanwhile, five of the 109 trusteed locals—the "paper locals" in New York—had been dissolved by the time Hoffa took over as president in 1958. Of the 104 remaining trusteed locals, eight were dissolved or merged and the others returned to self-governing status before the 1961 convention. It is worth noting that, with the apparent approval of the Board of Monitors, at least five other locals were placed under trusteeship during the 1958–1961 period, clear evidence that the power of trusteeship is a normal function of union administration.[26]

The 1961 convention not only raised the local's per capita obligation to the International from 40 cents to $1 a month but raised the minimum monthly dues a local may levy from $3 to $5. At the same time, as we have noted, it voted to compel every local, whatever its current dues structure was, to increase it by another $1.[27] The extra dollar caused some concern among many delegates, not only because it would go into effect without a membership vote but also because it would force higher dues even in locals well able to afford the per capita increase. The convention then wrote into the constitution permission for the general executive board to delay the $5 minimum or the $1 increase "in extreme hardship cases," that is, where a competitive organizing situation or low-wage contracts made the delay desirable. (Hoffa later reported that locals sought "hardship" relief for some 60,000 members, and that the board agreed to allow gradual increases geared to anticipated wage raises.) [28] None of the "hardship" delays, incidentally, affected the local's obligation to remit the $1 monthly per capita tax. There was some apprehension at the convention that the compulsory $1 increase might violate the Landrum-Griffin law, and the general executive board was authorized to "amend, modify, or defer" the per capita increase (along with the pension plan and a scheduled increase in strike benefits) if the courts vetoed the original plan. However, a federal court in Washington upheld the legality of the mandatory increase.[29]

Although the International has never levied an assessment

on its members (in addition to normal per capita dues), the general executive board has had authority to do so since 1920. Under the present constitution, it may levy a $1 monthly assessment whenever the value of the union's assets (except real estate) sinks below $20,000,000, and may continue this until the value reaches $25,000,000.[30] With the additional dues income passed by the 1961 convention, such a contingency is unlikely in the near future.

A pension plan for local union officers and employes has been a subject of discussion since 1952 and was approved in principle by the 1957 convention. Under the 1961 resolution, it would be financed and administered by the International Union. Beneficiaries would become eligible after three years of employment with past service retroactive to 1956. The basic amount of retirement benefit, at the age of 60 with 20 years of service, would consist of $1\frac{1}{4}$ per cent of average annual earnings up to 20 years and 2 per cent for each year past 20 with a 45 per cent maximum. Reduced pensions can be paid in cases of early retirement at 55 or disability at 45, with a death benefit prior to retirement set at two-thirds of contributions. Withdrawal benefits before retirement similarly are one-half of contributions during the first 10 years and two-thirds subsequently. All benefits are in addition to social security payments and receipts from other plans, including employer-financed pensions.[31]

Before 1961, the constitution required that all local unions deposit their funds "in reliable banks." Because several of Hoffa's financial dealings in depositing union funds in noninterest bank accounts had been questioned by his critics, the 1961 convention made clear that union funds could be deposited "in noninterest bearing commercial accounts, savings accounts, and safety deposit boxes," and it also permitted investments in real and personal property. All local union officers, business representatives, and others who handle funds and property must be "suitably bonded;" the constitution, in addition to requiring annual public audits of local union books, authorizes either the general president or general secretary-treasurer to order a further audit "at any time to the extent that he may determine." [32]

The International Union is obligated under the constitution to pay benefits in case of sanctioned strikes or declared lockout. Any member on strike or lockout is eligible, provided that his local union is not more than a month in arrears in its per capita payments and his own dues are similarly current. So long as the union's net worth is more than $33,000,000 (or $5,000,000 less than its assets in 1957), benefits are payable at $15 a week for the second through the fifth week and $25 a week for the sixth week and thereafter. Benefits are payable not only to members on strike or lockout but to any members made idle indirectly by a Teamsters strike. The general executive board is authorized "to pay out the entire International treasury to a local union that is on strike." However, the general president, with the approval of three-fourths of the executive board, and after a hearing, is empowered to cut off benefits "when satisfied upon facts and information that the support of a strike or lockout should cease." [33] The $25 strike benefit was added by the 1961 convention, and Hoffa estimated it would increase the union's benefit payments, which amounted to $1,748,006 during 1960, by another $1,500,000.[34]

To guard against improper payments, strikes involving 200 or fewer members require the general president's sanction. In these cases, locals anticipating strike action must fill out a questionnaire in quintuplicate, indicate what issues are in dispute, and state current working conditions, involvement of other unions, details on bargaining conferences, federal and state mediation efforts, and the nature of the strike vote. Copies are submitted simultaneously to the International office, the vice-president in the area, the area conference, and the joint council. After all intermediate bodies approve, the local union's account is checked to ascertain that it is in good standing. If all provisions have been complied with, the local union is notified that sanction has been granted, and the secretary-treasurer's office is alerted for payment of the benefits. Hoffa as general president is not personally involved except for a routine memorandum notifying him that sanction has been granted. However, in cases involving 200 or more members, approval of the general executive board is required and, given the size and strategic significance of a possible walkout, Hoffa may intervene either personally or by assigning the area vice-president or a general organizer to assist in settlement.

The constitution expressly forbids strikes or work stoppages when local unions are quarreling over jurisdiction; they must submit the issue to the joint council for decision, and they have a subsequent right of appeal to the general president and general executive board. Strikes also are prohibited among public employe members if they have been forbidden by law. A two-thirds majority of affected workers, voting by secret ballot, is necessary to call a strike. A simple majority can ratify a proposed settlement and, if the local executive board submits a contract proposal as the employer's "final offer," only a two-thirds majority can reject it. A lesser majority automatically empowers the local executive board to accept the proposal or negotiate additional provisions.[35]

Where the area conference bylaws require it, a local union must submit its contract demands to the joint council and conference for approval before opening negotiations with the employer. This procedure is mandatory in cases "where the proposed contract is for operations already subject to an area-wide agreement or a prospective area-wide agreement." In addition, in cases where a proposed contract would establish substandard wages or working conditions, the general executive board may order the local not to execute the agreement.[36]

The regulations in the constitution governing trials of locals and individual members are of paramount importance. Much of the present constitutional language on this subject was inserted by the 1940 convention, and some significant revisions were made at later assemblies, especially one which halted the appeal process at the general executive board for individual members and officers of local unions and subordinate bodies. Charges may be brought by either a fellow member of the local union or a member of another local. The local executive board serves as the trial board, except that it may decline to do so if the accuser is not a member of the local, but such a decision is subject to appeal to the joint council and the general executive board. If either the accuser or the accused is a local officer, "a disinterested member" must act as his substitute on the trial board. The charges, in writing, must specify the nature of the alleged offense and must be served upon the accused at least ten days before trial. The charged member may appear in his own defense and bring witnesses, but neither the prosecution nor defense may use nonmembers as counsel. The form of reporting the proceedings is left to the discretion of the trial board.[37]

The constitution lists a series of acts for which the accused must face trial—violation of a constitutional provision, violation of the oath of loyalty to the union, embezzlement, secession or fostering secession, abuse of fellow members and officers, and filing charges in bad faith or out of malice. In addition, a member may be accused of working at a plant that is on strike, informing an unfair employer "for the purpose of assisting such employer, or for any gain or promise of gain," and working for a firm on the union's unfair list without permission.[38] The 1961 convention deleted from this list such grounds as "gross disloyalty, or conduct unbecoming a member," "gross inefficiency" in the case of an officer, and a general charge of "activities which tend to bring the union into disrepute."

If found guilty, the accused is subject to such penalties as the trial board may direct—there are no specific penalties for specific offenses. The penalties may consist of "reprimands, fines, suspensions, expulsions, revocations, denial to hold any office permanently or for fixed period, or commands to do or perform or refrain from doing or performing specific acts." Pending a final decision on appeal, the decision must be complied with, unless the general president or general executive board waives immediate compliance.[39]

An appeal from the trial board's finding can be taken to the joint council and from there to the general executive board. Except for trials involving the subordinate bodies themselves (as in jurisdictional disputes) or elected international officers, there can be no further appeal. Any appeal must be taken within fifteen days of the decision and the appellate body may hear it either on the previous record or by a retrial. There is no fixed date for either the appellate hearing or the decision, except that the hearing must proceed without unnecessary delay" and a decision must be rendered "as promptly as possible." The trial board or any appellate body may name a fact-finding panel of disinterested members to hear the evidence and submit a report, including findings and recommendations, but the final decision must be made by the board itself.[40]

Similar provisions apply to charges against a local union where the joint council executive board serves as the trial board. Similarly, the general executive board tries a joint council under charges, as it does elected International officers. Appeals in these cases, as noted, can be taken to the convention. The general executive board may find an elected International officer guilty by a two-thirds vote of the entire board.[41]

The general executive board has jurisdiction over any trial of members or subordinate bodies charged with offenses committed against the international officers or the international union. The general president is empowered to assume original jurisdiction, at his discretion, whenever charges "involve or relate to a situation imminently dangerous to the welfare" of the union. In both cases, assumption of jurisdiction at the international level voids the jurisdiction of lower bodies. The general president may intervene through a deputy but the decision must be made by the general president himself and it is subject to appeal to the general executive board.[42]

The constitutional protections for a charged member are

not as strong as those contained in the model local bylaws proposed by the Board of Monitors. These bylaws provided that "the essential requirements of due process of law shall be observed" and that the charges must include sufficient detail to allow adequate defense, including dates and places where possible. "There shall be a presumption of innocence in favor of the accused," the model bylaws declared, and "clear and convincing evidence must be presented to support the charge." In addition, the trial board must furnish the accused with a summary of the testimony and evidence and, on request, prepare and furnish a verbatim record at cost. Finally, all proceedings in the case must be kept available until final disposition. But, as we have noted, the model bylaws, although recommended by the general executive board, were not mandatory and the form of recommendation did not encourage acceptance.

There are other areas where the union's judicial procedures, as outlined in the constitution, are subject to criticism. There is a failure to assure a truly independent trial board, the specific offenses subject to trial are vaguely worded, no attempt is made to relate specific penalties to specific offenses, and there is the possibility that the appellate process (which bars outside intervention while a decision is pending) may be long and drawn out. The use of a public review board, composed of nonunion members, to sit in independent judgment on the union's judicial practices apparently is out of the question in view of the union's experiences with the Board of Monitors.

The 1961 convention gave the general executive board authority to carve out new locals from existing organizations and, perhaps more to the point, "power to merge local unions and other subordinate bodies." [43] The latter provision aims to destroy the continued autonomy of small, ineffective locals, and Hoffa foreshadowed the convention action in 1958 when he told the Eastern Conference that "it is going to be necessary to review individual charters and see whether they are organizing their jurisdiction, or whether they are taking the position that they have a little kingdom all their own." [44] Such a step, of course, is a direct negation of Tobin's conception of a loose congregation of independent, autonomous locals, but it is essential to the building of a tightly controlled, powerful International leadership.

Unlike the constitutions of many other unions, the Teamsters constitution permits legal secession or disaffiliation—if the local and its members can pass through a maze of barbed-wire impediments against such action. For many years, the constitution merely repeated the traditional "rule of seven," that "no local union can dissolve while there are seven dissenting members." The 1952 convention extended the rule to cover secession or disaffiliation but provided that "all property, funds and assets, both real and personal," should then revert to the International. The 1957 convention then defined the rule in such a manner as to make secession virtually impossible. It explained the rule this way: "To ascertain whether or not seven members desire to retain the charter, there shall be subtracted from the complete membership list for the current month the name of each member in good standing who has, during the current month, submitted to the general secretary-treasurer a personally signed, notarized, individual affidavit attesting to his desire to sever his membership in the local union and the International Union. Such affidavit shall be forwarded to the general secretary-treasurer in the month for which it is signed. It shall be conclusively presumed that all who have not executed such individual affidavits still desire to retain the charter." [45]

The inability of a seceding local to follow these complicated instructions does not mean, of course, that the local cannot leave the international by utilizing National Labor Relations Board elections to shift bargaining rights from one union to another. Nor does the constitutional clause constitute an absolute legal bar to secession. In 1960, for instance, a Hawaii court held that a brewery local there, which had reserved the right to subsequent disaffiliation when it joined the Teamsters in 1947, could affiliate legally with the Brewery Workers Union, along with its funds and property.[46] The legal effectiveness of the secession clause was put in doubt after the 1961 convention when a group of Cincinnati locals, unhappy over Hoffa's re-election, left the Teamsters to re-join the AFL-CIO. The action resulted in a court suit by the International to assert its right to some $370,000 in local union assets, and the issue is still being litigated.

8

Relationships

with Other Unions

For many years, the relationship between the Teamsters Union and the American Federation of Labor was so matter-of-fact that there was no authority in the Teamsters' constitution for either affiliation with or independence of a national labor center. Until expulsion forced a change, the constitution merely set forth the mechanics of electing delegates to AFL or AFL-CIO conventions, provided for payment of expenses, insisted that the delegation cast its vote as a unit, and instructed the delegates to report to the general executive board and, by a written report in the monthly journal, to the general membership. When the AFL-CIO expelled the Teamsters in 1957, it broke off a relationship which had gone back to the very founding of the union.

More than most unions, the Teamsters owes its life to the help it received from the AFL when it was undergoing the splits and secession movements which nearly strangled it in infancy. Other AFL affiliates had fathered the central organization or had joined it as full-grown, mature organizations, but when George Innis showed up as the Team Drivers International Union's lone delegate to the AFL convention in 1899 (perhaps because it was in Detroit, his home town), he cast an insignificant 17 votes.[1] By 1938, the Teamsters was the largest union in the federation, and it maintained this commanding position even within the merged AFL-CIO. But, in the early days, the AFL executive council and Sam Gompers, the AFL president, kept a fatherly eye on the infant Teamsters organization. The AFL's mediatory efforts were decisive in sponsoring the amalgamated convention in 1903 of the Team Drivers and Teamsters National Union, and Gompers reported to his convention that year that AFL organizers had organized 75 local unions and turned them over to the Teamsters—"the largest single union gain" reported to the convention.[2] Dan Tobin did not serve as a delegate to AFL conventions until after he was elected Teamsters president. But his canny sense of organization politics soon found him choosing sides—usually the victorious one—in the bitter struggle within the AFL. Entering the "holy city" of the AFL's inner circle was not a simple task, Tobin confessed later, because "the old Gompers machine was insurmountable and impregnable," but the young Boston politician accomplished it.[3] By 1912, he was a member of the Gompers team, and he nominated the veteran leader for re-election when the Socialists made their bid for leadership under Max Hayes.[4]

But Tobin did not hesitate to play on both sides of the street. In 1917, he was the candidate of anti-administration forces to unseat John B. Lennon, the AFL's veteran treasurer, although Lennon had played a leading role in healing the Teamsters split fifteen years before. "In spite of the greatest machine that ever was inside the AFL," as Tobin boasted later, the Teamsters' president won an astounding 13,478 to 9,102 victory.[5] By 1921, Tobin was back with Gompers and supported him against John L. Lewis. But Tobin continued to be obstreperous and troublesome within the AFL. He resigned his post as AFL treasurer in a huff in 1928 when the executive council refused to endorse Alfred E. Smith, the Democratic candidate for president.[6] After sulking for six years, he returned to AFL leadership in 1934, and, as the representative of the federation's largest union, again began throwing his weight around. An observer's judgment that Tobin "bossed the executive council with shameless arrogance" was echoed by John English, the Teamsters secretary-treasurer, who remarked nostalgically that "he ran the AFL like it was his very own." [7] But Tobin was never able to win the recognition he sought as William Green's successor as AFL president. Perhaps it was, as John L. Lewis put it, because the Teamsters' chief was "one who has quarreled more and has derided the members of the executive council more than any one man in the American labor movement." [8]

One of Tobin's most frustrating periods on the AFL executive council came after 1935 when, despite his own craft leanings, he strove to prevent the CIO split, then labored to heal the breach. During this period, Tobin served the purposes of the Democratic administration's need for labor unity more often than he followed his own convictions. Indeed, he apparently had nothing but contempt for the CIO organizations, and he once described the CIO's membership as "rubbish." [9] But he urged a temporary relaxation of craft jurisdiction when the CIO drives got under way, and during the critical summer of 1936 he opposed the move to suspend the charters of the industrial unions.[10] From 1939 until 1950, he served on various AFL committees which sought to write a unity agreement with their CIO counterparts, but when unity was finally achieved Tobin was too old and had been replaced by a younger man.

Tobin was intensely loyal to the AFL when the split erupted into organizational warfare, although in 1930 he had sneered at Green as "a man who wore petticoats." [11] In 1941, he forbade Teamsters locals from cooperating "in any way" with CIO unions. He was bitter about what he considered ingratitude on the part of CIO unions which had been ready enough to turn toward the Teamsters when they needed help. The action of the Newspaper Guild in backing the CIO was especially galling because Tobin recalled that the Teamsters had helped the Guild win a crucial strike in Seattle. "We shall watch our step the next time they are in trouble," Tobin warned.[12]

The record is clear that Tobin regarded the AFL executive council more as a vehicle for his own internal political ambitions and a prop to the Democratic party he so loved, rather than as spokesman for the national labor movement. His contempt for the AFL was expressed partially in his open flouting of the federation's dues requirements. From 1946 to 1953, he kept the Teamsters' per capita payments level at 625,000 to 650,000 members, although the union's actual membership grew from 765,000 to 1,200,000. Despite this disdain, Tobin always saw to it that he headed the Teamsters' delegation to the AFL convention and served as its spokesman. Indeed, one of the conditions he demanded before he agreed to retire as Teamsters president was a constitutional provision that the president emeritus (the title he assumed) would automatically serve as an AFL delegate. Except for the general president and the general secretary-treasurer, the other members of the AFL convention delegation often were lesser officials without power or prestige; as Tobin explained, they "get a few days' pay and usually say nothing." [13]

Tobin did not hesitate to use his power on the executive council to advance the Teamsters' interests vis-a-vis other unions. The executive council bowed submissively to his demands that the union's jurisdiction be broadened to include first the warehousemen, then the cannery workers, gas station attendants, and grain processors. Even more important was the virtually unbroken record of executive council decisions favoring the Teamsters in jurisdictional disputes. In most cases, it was Tobin's political alliances with other council members which induced a pro-Teamsters decision over unions which had both tradition and members to justify their jurisdictional claims.

The Teamsters' command over the commercial trucking industry gave it an advantage over other unions because of its ability to affect strikes by inside workers. A decision by the Teamsters to observe picket lines or cross them often spelled victory or defeat in a hard-fought strike. Tobin was not unaware of this power and wanted to manipulate it by keeping a veto power over its use. He urged his members to seek permission from the International before observing a picket line, complaining that "many unions depend on us to organize for them." [14] "We are strongly opposed to our members stopping at every picket line," he once explained. "We touch on every trade and industry and we'd have our boys tied up most of the time." [15] But Tobin's control was subject to the wishes of the local officers and of the drivers themselves, who generally adhered to a strict policy of honoring picket lines. Nevertheless, Beck illustrated the Teamsters' awesome power to kill a strike in 1947 when he ordered Teamsters to go through pickets established by the Retail Clerks in Los Angeles.[16] In contrast, the Senate committee testimony disclosed that a refusal to cross a Barbers' picket line could force the giant Waldorf-Astoria hotel to insist that its barber shop sign with the union.[17]

Even after the Teamsters were ousted from the AFL-CIO, their support aided AFL-CIO unions on strike or, conversely, lack of Teamsters support diminished chance of success. Hoffa noted in 1959 that a strike by airline stewardesses against Lake Central Airlines was won with Teamsters' support, although members of the stewardesses' parent union, the Air Line Pilots Association, continued to fly.[18] Another indication of how this power could be manipulated was noted during a strike in Detroit by an independent mailers union which halted publication of the city's newspapers. Officials of the International Typographical Union complained that the Teamsters were supporting the picket line in order to dictate to the other printing crafts.[19] The Landrum-Griffin law with its severe penalties against secondary boycotts (including a refusal to cross a picket line by an employe of an outside carrier) served to enervate much of this strength. Hoffa announced shortly after the law was passed that the union would honor striking picket lines of other unions only if "the striking unions will guarantee the Teamsters against any possible loss through lawsuits, governmental action, or any other expense." [20]

Many of the Teamsters' jurisdictional quarrels date back to the early days of the AFL. The nature of the union's jurisdiction made inevitable constant friction between the Teamsters and other tunions. Its authority over drivers, later broadened to include loading dock workers and then shipping room employes behind the docks, allowed the Teamsters to cut across the jurisdiction of almost every other union. There was no argument about drivers or dock employes of commercial trucking firms, but conflict began when these workers were hired by companies whose other employes came under a separate jurisdiction. Not all problems were as susceptible to easy solution as that in the dairy industry where no union claimed membership among the inside employes, permitting the Teamsters to assume jurisdiction without protest.

One of the most notable and persistent jurisdictional quarrels in American labor history is that between the Teamsters and Brewery Workers. The Brewery Workers, chartered by the AFL in 1887—more than a decade before the Teamsters—had been given jurisdiction over all workers in the industry. But the AFL grant of jurisdiction to the Team Drivers over all drivers contradicted the previous award and the issue was joined. The AFL then issued a number of contradictory decisions—in 1900 in favor of the Brewery Workers, in 1907 in favor of the Teamsters, and in 1913 in favor of the Brewery Workers. The advent of prohibition forced a truce, but open warfare was renewed after repeal revived the Brewery Workers as a potent force. By 1933, however, Tobin could dictate AFL policy and did, asserting anew the Teamsters' denied claim over beer truck drivers. The controversy was a bitter one and each side used its full economic force to safeguard its claimed jurisdiction, although the Teamsters, it should be noted, went even farther and supplied inside workers in cases where the Brewery Workers had struck. The Brewery Workers sought the protection of civil courts in its claim and secured an injunction against the AFL's decision, but this was reversed by a higher court. The warfare spread after the 1941 AFL convention suspended the Brewery Workers union, and the Teamsters discarded any pretense that it recognized the other union's claim to the inside brewers and bottlers. It continued with unabated force even after the Brewery Workers again became a coaffiliate with the Teamsters in the AFL-CIO and, of course, after the AFL-CIO ousted the Teamsters.[21]

There were other jurisdictional quarrels over the years. A dispute with the Iron Workers about which union would assert jurisdiction over the moving of heavy machinery finally was settled in 1925, but the resulting disharmony stalled Teamsters affiliation with the AFL building trades department until 1928. During the prolonged debate P. J. Morrin, president of the Iron Workers, at one time protested Tobin's use of his position as a member of the AFL executive council to determine the issue.[22] Another dispute, still alive, concerns railway express drivers and dates back to 1903. An AFL decision in 1924 awarding jurisdiction to the Teamsters, as against a claim by the Brotherhood of Railway Clerks, was so distasteful to the affected drivers that 18,000 of them seceded and formed an independent union. A truce was finally agreed upon by which the Teamsters represented express drivers in eight cities and the Railway Clerks got the rest, but neither side was content with half a loaf and the controversy has never died down.[23] Early efforts by the Bakery and Confectionery Workers to follow the example of the Brewery Workers and assert jurisdiction over bakery drivers were beaten back by Tobin without much difficulty, despite the fact that many of the drivers had joined the inside union. A similar edict by the AFL convention cemented Teamsters jurisdiction over laundry drivers. Other disputes through the years concerned jurisdiction over bus drivers (both with the Street Railway Employes and Railroad Trainmen), over operators of ready-mix concrete carriers (with the Operating Engineers), and over workers in stockrooms in retail establishments (with the Retail Clerks).[24] In almost all cases, the Teamsters ended up on top.

A jurisdictional controversy arising out of the shift from horse-drawn cartage to motor trucking was settled by a compromise in 1926 when the Teamsters and the International Association of Machinists agreed to divide the work. The Machinists union was granted jurisdiction over the auto mechanics, and the Teamsters was given the less skilled workers. However, Tobin obviously chafed at the limitations, especially after the growth of the trucking industry expanded Teamsters power, and he was quick to cancel it in 1943 when the Machinists (involved in an unrelated dispute) withdrew from the AFL. (It is worth recalling, in view of Hoffa's protests in 1958 when the AFL-CIO ordered its affiliates to cancel mutual assistance pacts with the Teamsters, that Tobin had supplied the precedent for such exclusions.) [25] The garage dispute was overshadowed, however, by a major break between the two unions during a Machinists strike at the Boeing aircraft plant in Seattle in 1948. Beck used the strike as an excuse to assert jurisdiction over "warehousemen" employed by Boeing, insisting that some 5,000 of Boeing's 14,000 employes were included in this elastic classification. He organized a separate local and began a membership drive inside the plant while the Machinists were picketing at the gates. When the strikers expressed a natural resentment at such activities, despite its compliant endorsement by the AFL executive council, Beck scornfully demanded jurisdiction over the production workers as well. His claim was rejected by the workers, who voted for the Machinists by a two-to-one margin. But the scars remain. The Teamsters local, incidentally, has been kept alive despite the election defeat and, after 13 years of trusteeship under Frank Brewster, it was declared self-governing in 1961.[26]

Not all the relationships between the Teamsters and other unions were quarrelsome. In many cases (including some where the Teamsters had emerged victorious in a jurisdictional dispute), the two sides joined in a mutual assistance pact, pledging cooperation in organizing and negotiating activities as well as jurisdictional peace. Such pacts were drawn with several of the building trades unions; the Meat Cutters, the Bakery Workers, the Upholsterers, and the Machinists. In almost all pacts of this nature, a joint committee was named to umpire the constantly recurring disputes. Many of these pacts continued in *de facto* operation on the local level long after the AFL-CIO expelled the Teamsters and ordered such documents cancelled.

George Meany, newly elected to AFL leadership in 1952, made the achievement of labor unity the first order of business. As the first major step in this direction, AFL and CIO committees agreed on a voluntary "no raiding" agreement by which each signatory union would respect the bargaining jurisdiction of all others. Dave Beck, sitting as a member of the AFL executive council, refused to sign the agreement, arguing that it would prohibit the Teamsters from recovering members in its proper jurisdiction lost to other unions. (Two examples of such losses, often cited by Beck, were New York laundry drivers who belonged to the Amalgamated Clothing Workers and Detroit dairy workers who have been organized by the United Auto Workers.)

But formal merger between the AFL and CIO in 1955 followed the "no raiding" pact, despite Beck's reluctance, and he prepared to make the most of the situation. By virtue of the Teamsters' huge membership, he sat on the AFL-CIO executive council and even joined the merged organization's Industrial Union Department, the stronghold of the former CIO unions, although he tried to cut the Teamsters' dues payments from 400,000 to a token 25,000.[27] But Beck was never to play a major role in AFL-CIO deliberations. Publicized scandals involving officers of the Laundry Workers, the Allied Industrial Workers, and the Distillery Workers forced the AFL-CIO executive council in the summer of 1956 to vest its ethical practices committee with power to investigate such cases. By 1957, when the Teamsters went before the Senate committee, the AFL-CIO position was clear, morally unobjectionable, and not subject to change. In direct violation of the AFL-CIO ethical practices codes, Beck used the fifth amendment freely in refusing to testify before the committee, and he was removed as an AFL-CIO vice-president. However, the AFL-CIO executive council still reserved a place for the Teamsters and (in obvious ignorance of Teamsters' internal politics) replaced Beck with John English, the union's secretary-treasurer who, although a bitter foe of Beck, was one of Hoffa's principal supporters.

The Senate committee, meanwhile, had finished with Beck and turned its attention to Hoffa. As the testimony mounted up, the AFL-CIO ethical practices committee, headed by Al J. Hayes of the Machinists, returned its own indictment of the Teamsters, based almost wholly on material which had been presented before the Senate group. Shortly before the Teamsters convention, the AFL-CIO group held formal hearings on the charges, and Hoffa made a detailed reply. It was an attempt at point-by-point refutation of the committee's charges, some of it delivered in an off-the-record session during which Hoffa discussed his controversial relations with particular individuals. The committee was not impressed with his defense, commenting at one point that "if Vice-President Hoffa believes his statement, we can attribute it only to his insensitivity to the most elementary principles of trade union morality." [28] The executive council accordingly ordered the union "to remove and bar from any position or office, either appoinitive or elective, in the International Union or any of its subordinate bodies, those who are responsible for these abuses." The council subsequently modified its ultimatum to demand that the Teamsters merely "remove and bar from office in the International Union," but, in either case, it made clear that it did not consider Hoffa fit for the union's presidency.[29]

The Teamsters convention, which met shortly after the first ultimatum, reacted in utter defiance. It not only elected Hoffa president, but named as new vice-presidents John O'Rourke of New York and Owen (Bert) Brennan of Detroit, both of whom had invoked the fifth amendment to avoid testifying. After some reluctance, the Teamsters leaders agreed to read the AFL-CIO report to the delegates, but the convention expunged the document from its proceedings and rejected a motion to undertake its own investigation of the charges. The defiance left the AFL-CIO leaders no alternative but to recommend the expulsion of its largest union from the ranks of the merged labor movement.[30] The Teamsters kept alive a vain hope that the unions it had befriended in the past would come to its rescue and lobbied in opposition to the executive council's report. The hope flickered momentarily when the Building Trades Department unanimously passed a resoultion deploring the proposed expulsion. But the verdict was inevitable. Gibbons charged later that "a lot of people in the AFL-CIO were very scared when the investigation came along" and "the expulsion was largely a case of throwing Teamsters to the dogs in the hope that they might avoid further heat themselves." [31] Whatever the reasons, the council secured its two-thirds majority with ease. Expulsion was voted by an overwhelming majority of 10,-458,598 to 2,266,497. (Even if the Teamsters with their 1,330,000 members and four other suspended unions with some 300,000 more had voted, the two-thirds majority would have been secured.) Only 21 unions voted for the Teamsters, and some of them, like the International Typographical Union, were not pro-Teamsters but objected to the exercise of the expulsion power. Only four unions voting against expulsion had memberships greater than 100,000. Significantly, of 124 delegates from city central bodies recorded on the vote, only 53 voted in favor of expulsion while 35 voted against it and 36 abstained—a tribute to the regard which the Teamsters held at the local level.[32]

Hoffa was prepared to turn the other cheek when expulsion came. Upon his election as Teamsters' president, he had pledged that "the Teamsters will never fire the first shot in a civil war in the American labor movement." [33] In the months which followed expulsion, he was careful not to disassociate himself and the Teamsters any more than necessary from the merged labor movement. Gibbons, who had become Hoffa's executive assistant, said that the truck union would "do nothing to draw the Teamsters and the federation apart." [34] The mutual aid pacts with other AFL-CIO unions were kept alive—even with the Machinists whose president, Al Hayes, had been one of Hoffa's chief prosecutors. By May, Hoffa was ready to make a bold move to retain status in the labor movement despite ouster. In simultaneous announcements, he disclosed that peace talks were under way with two traditional rivals—the Brewery Workers and the Retail Clerks. These talks had been preceded a week earlier by an agreement for a mutual organizing campaign with the Office Employes, which once had haled the Teamsters into court for refusing to let Teamsters' clerical help join a union of their choice.[35] At the same time, negotiations were in progress with two maritime unions to establish the Conference on Transportation Unity. Hoffa's strategy was apparent. If he could not stay within the AFL-CIO, he was prepared to achieve the same objective through separate alliances with individual unions, even with jurisdictional foes.

Meany reacted with characteristic decisiveness. "Any alliance," he asserted, "to build up the strength and prestige of (ousted) unions is out," although he said day-to-day working arrangements on a local basis were permissible.[36] Meany followed through when the AFL-CIO executive council met with an order declaring that any alliance, formal or informal, "is in direct contradiction to both the spirit and the letter of our constitution" and directed that these alliances be cancelled. However, the order again excepted "situations which arise in the day-to-day relationships between various workers which would call for understanding and cooperation based on elementary trade union principles between these workers at the local level." [37] Meany's orders to quarantine the Teamsters coincided with the aggressive campaign by the Board of Monitors against Hoffa's leadership. It was obvious that Hoffa's pacificatory policy, as far as top AFL-CIO officialdom was concerned, had brought neither reconciliation nor cooperation.

Hoffa bowed to the edict and agreed to cancel the mutual aid pacts "to avoid embarrassing" his union's friends within the AFL-CIO, although he remarked bitterly that "out of little men come big demands." "There wasn't one single president of those international unions," he insisted, "who were desirous on their own of cancelling those pacts." The Teamsters board empowered Hoffa and English to work out "memoranda of understanding" as substitutes for more formal alliances and pledged continued cooperation at the local level.[38] "Surely the CIO-AFL (sic) executive council knows that it cannot throw the Teamsters out of the labor movement," Hoffa reported to the Central Conference of Teamsters. "They can force removal of our representatives from the councils of city, state, and international federations, but actual trade union work is done at the local level, not in the chambers of top-level representatives. A million and one-half workers cannot be isolated from the main body of labor." [39]

Meanwhile, Hoffa resorted to bitter personal attacks on Meany, whom he blamed for the widening of the gap. He charged that the AFL-CIO president had forsaken his role as labor leader for "acceptance" by the community. "It's fine to wear a tuxedo to a banquet, to be a United Nations representative," he declared, "but this is not a birthright." Hoffa demanded that his AFL-CIO foe stop "seeking respectability above all else." "He may have to quit a few country clubs," he said, "he may have to forego the dubious distinction of being invited to address employers' groups." [40] Any hope for personal reconciliation vanished in the exchange of invective. Walter Reuther, the former CIO president, was another target for Hoffa's anger. "We have friends in Solidarity House (UAW headquarters)," Hoffa said, "and we know each and every day many of the things that are supposed to be top secret." Reuther retorted that Hoffa "should be put in jail along with his associates," and Hoffa denounced a contract settlement between the UAW and the auto industry as "a political sellout." [41]

The Teamsters, however, were successful in maintaining cordial local relations and, as an observer later remarked, "mutual assistance pacts had to be written in invisible ink on impalpable paper, but the ties between the truckers and the unions that need their help remained as firm as before." [42] But the failure of Hoffa's "live and let live" strategy was soon reflected in an aggressive organizing campaign which did not avoid direct conflicts with AFL-CIO unions. AFL-CIO central bodies obeyed Meany's edict and closed their doors to the Teamsters, while men like William A. Lee, a former Teamsters vice-president, resigned as president of a Teamsters bakery drivers local so that he could continue as president of the Chicago Federation of Labor.[43] By the time the 1959 AFL-CIO convention met, Hoffa was ready to make another try at rapprochement. The Painters Union national convention adopted a resolution calling for the Teamsters readmission, and so did important state federations in Pennsylvania and Illinois as well as a number of city central bodies.[44] But the AFL-CIO convention referred the Painters' resolution to the executive council without discussion, and the Teamsters remained in exile.

Nevertheless, there were two convention episodes which gave the Teamsters some hope. One came when Meany, replying to a demand that the AFL-CIO establish a rival Teamsters union, replied that "it is not the part of wisdom to attempt to charter a new Teamsters union." [45] Although Hickey had predicted before Hoffa's election that the Teamsters would lose two-thirds of its members if it left the AFL-CIO, Meany reported to the convention that there had been no serious revolt within the Teamsters and that any dissident elements could be "destroyed" within twenty-four hours. A more significant event, from the Teamsters' point of view, was passage by the convention of a resolution denouncing the McClellan committee as "little more than a vehicle of reactionary elements seeking to discredit the American labor movement." Hoffa quickly made it clear that he regarded the AFL-CIO resolution as negating the original report of the AFL-CIO committee on ethical practices, since the AFL-CIO group had based its indictment of the Teamsters almost wholly on the testimony before the Senate committee.[46]

An uneasy truce governed relationships between the Teamsters and AFL-CIO unions during the next two years while Hoffa centered his efforts on ridding his union of the monitors and securing court approval for a new convention. The 1961 convention then set the stage for a two-front campaign to get back in the AFL-CIO. It amended the constitution to give the general executive board authority "to enter into agreement and arrangements for the purpose of effectuating the affiliation of the International Union, or its coordination with other national or international organizations or federation of labor organizations, committees, or multi-union conferences, and also for the purpose of creating and/or participating in any federation of labor organizations."[47] Thus, the Teamsters could either rejoin the AFL-CIO, "coordinate" with it, or seek to create a separate federation.

Hoffa immediately put this strategy into practice. On the one hand, he threatened the AFL-CIO with formation of a dual federation and gave it eighteen months to readmit the Teamsters or break up. He denounced Meany as the "sole obstacle" to reaffiliation, referring to the AFL-CIO leader as "that dopey, thick-headed Irishman."[48] On the other hand, Teamsters began an intensive lobbying effort at AFL-CIO "grass roots" levels, especially among the friendly building trades, to support an invitation to come back. The AFL-CIO retaliated by encouraging a group of Teamsters locals in

Cincinnati, long an anti-Hoffa stronghold, to leave the Teamsters—the first major defection from Hoffa's leadership. The influential voice of Secretary of Labor Arthur Goldberg, who had been counsel to the AFL-CIO ethical practices committee, joined the anti-Teamster clamor when he declared that "my attitude toward Hoffa is the same as it was—I have not changed my mind." [49] When the AFL-CIO council met in October, it was faced with two contrary proposals. Joseph Curran, a member of the ethical practices committee who nevertheless continued to maintain cordial relations with Hoffa, proposed that a committee be established to work for the Teamsters' reaffiliation. James Carey of the International Union of Electrical Workers and Joseph Beirne of the Communication Workers urged the formation of a dual Teamsters union.

The executive council avoided either extreme. It agreed to charter as an AFL-CIO affiliate any Teamsters local which rejected Hoffa's leadership, but it avoided any commitment to sponsor a rival union which would challenge Hoffa on the nation's highways. Meany, however, made clear that he was ready to take on Hoffa, whom he labeled "unfit to head a trade union." "There is every indication," Meany declared, "that the (Teamsters) Union is more than ever under the influence of corrupt elements." [50] Meany told reporters that the AFL-CIO had on hand applications from 100 of the 900 Teamsters locals for a separate charter, but it became obvious as the months passed that most of these came from dissident groups within locals rather than the locals themselves. Some of the Cincinnati locals were absorbed by the Brewery Workers, and a Chicago taxi local, which had revolted against Joseph Glimco, a Hoffa supporter, joined the Seafarers Union. But there was little indication that Meany had been wrong in 1959 when he warned against the futility of fighting Hoffa on his home grounds.

With Meany's adamant opposition to reaffiliation, it was obvious that the Teamsters' campaign to return to the AFL-CIO was doomed to failure—at least at the 1961 convention.

The powerful Building Trades Department, which had opposed the original expulsion edict, backtracked from its stand to propose a condition-weighted resolution which would require "complete observance" by the Teamsters of AFL-CIO "rules, laws, standards, and policies." This was again watered down by the convention to a general statement on reaffiliation, satisfactory to both sides to such a degree that it passed without dissent.[51]

Hoffa continued his two-front campaign. Despite the apparently negative resolution, he insisted that it was the basis for reaffiliation, and the union's magazine announced that "the International Brotherhood of Teamsters was invited to make application for membership in the AFL-CIO." It described the convention action as a "response to the tremendous grass roots demand for the return of the Teamsters" and charged that reporters had "misinterpreted" its meaning.[52] Hoffa announced that the Teamsters would be back in the AFL-CIO "in the foreseeable future" and said he was ready to initiate talks toward this end.[53] At the same time, however, the Teamsters general executive board laid the groundwork for a potential dual federation by "affiliating" the 60,000-member Laundry Workers Union, also expelled from the AFL-CIO, to the Teamsters.

The authority for such a step was contained in a new article written into the Teamsters 1961 constitution which empowered the board to make separate dues arrangements for unions which would associate with the Teamsters but not merge with it. Under the board's action, the Laundry Workers Union would keep its autonomy and officers and pay a 5-cent per capita monthly tax (instead of the $1 paid by regular Teamsters locals). Laundry Workers delegates could participate in meetings of Teamsters joint council but would forego voting rights. Neither would members of the "affiliated" union participate in strike benefits, health and welfare plans, or pension arrangements open to Teamsters officers and members.[54] In effect, it would confer a form of legality upon the *de facto* relationship which long existed between the two unions—a relationship clearly recognized by President Ralph Fagan of the Laundry Workers when he saluted the Teamsters as his union's "big brothers." [55] The dominant position of the laundry drivers in the industry's labor relations had reduced the inside laundry union in many cities to a Teamsters satellite, and the new relationship did nothing to alter this. Certainly, the proposal gave the Laundry Workers little more than what it had enjoyed before—a kind of junior partnership, on sufferance, with little voice and no vote.

There was no doubt that Hoffa intended the "affiliation" of the Laundry Workers to serve a propaganda purpose. It was clear that he wanted the step to be interpreted as bringing closer the realization of his oft-threatened dual federation. Nevertheless, the action was charged with serious implications in the Teamsters' campaign to regain some measure of respectability and prestige. A new national labor center, if it were to attain its goals, necessarily had to be built around the building trades and those AFL-CIO unions which, even if they preferred Hoffa to Meany, enjoyed high public standing. But the Laundry Workers Union was no shining star which other unions might want to follow. Unlike the Teamsters, the Laundry Workers had been let off lightly by the McClellan Senate committee, but this was because earlier Senate investigators, especially the Douglas committee probing misuse of health and welfare funds, had dug deeply into its case. Along with the Allied Industrial Workers and the Distillery Workers, the Laundry Workers was the first order of business before the AFL-CIO ethical practices committee in May 1957.[56] The first two unions accepted AFL-CIO monitorship and were restored to good standing after convincing the AFL-CIO executive council that they abided by the labor movement's ethical standards. But the Laundry Workers Union rejected AFL-CIO suggestions for change and was expelled. There was sufficient dissension within it so that the AFL-CIO chartered a separate international, which attracted those locals that were unhappy with the Senate disclosures and the expulsion. But this had the paradoxical effect of keeping the rest of the union even more securely under the old discredited leadership—and it was this group with which Hoffa proposed to pioneer in a new labor center.

Hoffa relied on a more orthodox procedure when he sought to bring into the Teamsters' orbit another union expelled by the AFL-CIO—the Bakery and Confectionery Workers Union. Like the Laundry Workers, the bakers had rejected AFL-CIO conditions which might have averted expulsion, and the AFL-CIO set up a rival union. However, the old union remained divided over the issue, with a powerful group continuing to urge merger with the new AFL-CIO union and eventual reaffiliation with the AFL-CIO. Hoffa countered with a proposal that the Bakery Union merge with the Teamsters as a separate division, enjoying all the rights and privileges of membership. Despite his warning that a rejection of this proposal would leave the union open to Teamsters' raids, the Bakery Workers convention shunted it aside and elected a new leadership committed to the AFL-CIO. It was the most serious defeat Hoffa suffered since the expulsion.[57]

Expulsion from the AFL-CIO was instrumental in forcing the Teamsters to withdraw from the International Transport Workers Federation, a step which the union took with sincere reluctance. Tobin often served as an AFL delegate to world labor meetings while Beck, who had visions of being acclaimed a world statesman even as he was being shelved at home, established a branch office of the union in Vienna. Hoffa sought to continue close relations with transport unions abroad and, during the London bus strike in 1958, the Teamsters sent $5,000 as a token of sympathy to the powerful British Transport and General Workers Federation. Six Teamsters delegates, headed by Harold Gibbons, attended the world congress of the International Transport Workers Federation in the summer of 1958, and there were reports that Hoffa wanted a seat on the federation's execu-

tive board.[58] But the federation's executive committee decided instead to investigate the charges of corruption against
the Teamsters. The findings of the investigation were not
made public, and Hoffa told the Senate committee that "we
discussed the matter with Omar Becu (the federation's general secretary) and, because of the dissension, we withdrew."[59]

The Teamsters also ran into difficulties with the Canadian
Labor Congress, but the Canadians apparently acted for
reasons of their own without reference to the AFL-CIO expulsion. Shortly after the Teamsters Union was expelled,
Gordon Cushing, the Canadian executive vice-president,
indicated there would be no similar action by his organization, adding that "there have been no suggestions of improper practices on the part of any of the Canadian ranking
officers (of the Teamsters)." President Claude Jodoin even
appeared at the annual Canadian Teamsters Conference
meeting to reassure the delegates that the breach did not
extend north of the border.[60] But the Canadians reacted
vigorously when the Teamsters initiated a membership drive
among some 290 employes of a newly formed road transport
division of the Canadian Pacific Railway. The Brotherhood
of Railway Clerks, which held a national contract with the
railroad, complained that the Teamsters had invaded its
jurisdiction, and the Canadian Labor Congress expelled the
Teamsters after the truck union refused to comply with its
cease-and-desist order.[61]

The relationships between the Teamsters and other AFL-
CIO unions were not markedly affected by the AFL-CIO
expulsion, except for the formal cancellation of the mutual-
aid pacts already noted. As a general rule, cordial relationships were maintained with unions which had cooperated
in working agreements before expulsion, while disputes with
other unions dating back many years continued unabated.
After Hoffa's tentative offer of a peaceful settlement to the
Brewery Workers was negated by Meany's adverse reaction,
the two unions continued to clash repeatedly in organiza-

tional situations, and the Brewery Workers played a leading role in encouraging the Cincinnati rebellion. A bitter acrimony was engendered between the Teamsters and the Seafarers Union, which had cold-shouldered Hoffa's proposal for a Conference on Transportation Unity. The two unions met head-on in rival organizational drives in Puerto Rico, occasionally spilling blood in open street fighting. Paul Hall, president of the Seafarers, was one of Meany's strongest backers in 1961 in rebuffing Hoffa's drive to return to the AFL-CIO, describing Hoffa as "a fink from his very heart— he always has been and always will be." Hall, in a wide detour from his union's normal jurisdiction, granted Seafarers' charters to dissident taxi drivers groups in Chicago and St. Louis which had left the Teamsters, and Hoffa promptly announced that 3,200 members of the Seafarers' industrial division in Philadelphia had voted to join his union.[62] On the other hand, Teamsters' relationships with the Building Trades Department were so close that the AFL-CIO unit invited Teamsters locals to send delegates to the department's annual national legislative conference in 1962.[63]

Under Hoffa's leadership, the Teamsters Union has reversed its historic policy of adamant opposition to the leadership of Harry Bridges in the west coast International Longshoremen's and Warehousemen's Union—and, indeed, to other unions which have followed a pro-Communist line. The reasons for such a move are obscure and may well spring from the isolation into which expulsion from the AFL-CIO forced the Teamsters. Hoffa himself has insisted that Teamsters cooperation with Bridges grows out of "basic trade unionism" and is not linked to political considerations. It is certainly true that the two unions, faced with the blurring of normal jurisdictional lines because of increased mechanization in dock procedures, are committed to a natural alliance to prevent chaos on the waterfront. In a similar way, the Teamsters and the Mine, Mill, and Smelter Workers (another union expelled from the CIO as pro-Communist) have a mutual interest in clarifying the numerous organizational and jurisdictional problems which crop up in an area where both unions hold contracts. "The Longshoremen and the Teamsters both work on the docks, and we have mutual problems," Hoffa explained. "We are not interested in Bridges' politics—we are interested in avoiding jurisdictional conflict as automation takes over the docks." "I deal with Goldblatt (Bridges' secretary-treasurer) like our Secretary Herter deals with Khrushchev," Hoffa assured the Senate committee.[64]

But Hoffa has gone much farther than formal cooperation at the job level. Dave Beck's drive to destroy Bridges' union (which gave the Teamsters jurisdiction over warehousing and cannery processing, it will be recalled) was denounced by Hoffa as "the worst mistake ever made by the Teamsters," and Beck's denunciation of Bridges' pro-Communist views was ridiculed as "some phony contention." [65] Instead, Hoffa asserted that the Bridges union had been certified by the National Labor Relations Board, and that the government had failed to deport Bridges as a Communist. "The ILWU members have been called Communists; Teamsters have been called gangsters," Hoffa declared. "But I'd rather belong to either union than to one of those so-called clean unions headed by tired old men who have never been on a picket line in their lives." [66] The growing relationship was dramatized at the 1961 convention when Bridges, who once would have risked physical injury if he had appeared at a Teamsters gathering, showed up on the platform as an invited guest. Bridges responded by praising Hoffa as "one of the greatest, outspoken, and fighting labor leaders of this country" and acclaimed the Teamsters as "one of the greatest hopes of our country." [67]

Whatever may have motivated the Teamsters in this strange relationship, it was clear that the Communists were ready to accept Hoffa's leadership in a dual federation. George Morris, the labor editor of the Communist newspaper, *The Worker,* noted that "when Lewis appeared, some progressives couldn't conceive that anything good (might) come" and asked "will the Teamsters be the instrument to a new advance?" In later columns, he praised Hoffa and the Teamsters, and said of Gibbons' local in St. Louis that "such progressive leadership sets an example for the entire labor movement." [68] However, the United Electrical Workers, which has followed pro-Communist leadership, reportedly has rejected any formal alliance with the Teamsters, although it has accepted collaboration "in a common interest." [69]

9

The Future

The Teamsters Union, as we have seen, is neither the model of a democratic, idealistic unionism which stirs our hearts and hopes, nor the oppressive juggernaut which crushes beneath its flanged wheels any display of membership initiative or individual nonconformism. It is, in fact, a massive bureaucracy, making progress at the pace set by its general president but geared to the inherent powers of the local and regional leaders to slow it down whenever it moves too fast for them. The union has within it areas of infection—festering sores of racketeering and corruption which threaten to spread and devour the entire body. By the same token, it also has unions like St. Louis Local 688, which thrives on membership participation and provides a wide range of welfare services to its members in addition to accomplishing the economic gains of more routine unionism. But most of the union's locals are unimaginative, routine organizations which go about their daily chores without excitement or fervor. The average local commands neither the loyalty nor the hatred of its members and, except in times of crisis, it exists on indifference and apathy.

The basic problem the Teamsters Union presents is not that of the toleration of racketeering. It is that the union may well be the prototype of a developing unionism which soon may embrace the entire labor movement. Almost since the beginning, Teamsters leaders have been occupied with the virtues of business unionism—the concept that the unions are quasi-commercial organizations in American economic life, performing a necessary market function for their members in getting them the highest possible price for their labor. It is not very far from Dan Tobin's belief that the international union is "founded on business ethics and business principles," [1] to Dave Beck's declaration that "I run this office just like a business—just like an oil company or a railroad; our business is selling labor." [2] And it is only a step further to Frank Brewster, who explained that a union committee "functions the same as a board of directors in any big corporation; I do not believe that the stockholder always has the right to say how they are going to spend their money to make their business profitable." [3] Hoffa accepts this attitude as his own; the operation of a union is a business, and he is a businessman hired to run it in the best interests of the owners. "Everybody who writes about me seems amazed that I call it a business, instead of a crusade or something," he once told members of his home local. "Well, it is a business. We're not labor statesmen here. We're not humanitarians or longhairs. Look, what do you hire us for? Is it to throw a picnic for you? Is it to study the European situation? Or is it to sell your labor at the top dollar?" [4] On occasion, Hoffa will talk about the union and its "major responsibility to represent human values in the sweeping economic and technical changes that are taking place;" [5] but this is an intellectualized version of his belief that the union must continually perform for its members or face the possibility that the owners may insist on a change in management. "Unfortunately for the would-be modern-day reformers," he remarked, "workers do not behave in the manner their hazy theories presume. Most people do not want to participate in the day-to-day operations of their union—this is the business agent's job. But when people are really dissatisfied or hurt, watch out for the fireworks. A leader must deliver what the people really want." [6] Although he is fiercely loyal to the concept that the union must produce results for the members, Hoffa is openly contemptuous of the members' ability to pass on the complex details of the union's affairs. "The average worker should be but is not concerned," he said, "with the niceties of the legal language of his local union bylaws. He is not concerned with the details of accounting procedure." [7]

This attitude leads inevitably to the next stop along the road—the concept that the union member's concern is with his wages and hours, not with how the dues money is spent or whether the business agent is involved in a conflict of interest. "I will never agree that it is immoral or improper for a person to have outside interests as long as it does not affect his collective bargaining," Hoffa told the Senate committee.[8] These business interests could include firms with which the union had a contract, Hoffa admitted. "If they were paying the standard wage, hours, and conditions," he said, "I would not find any fault with it." Hoffa even went on to suggest that such an arrangement might be beneficial to the union's membership. "It is educational and beneficial," he explained, "for a business agent to be able to know as much or more about the employer's business at the bargaining table than the employer. And the only way he can find out the practices of an employer is to actually find that he (the business agent) has to meet a payroll."

But this is an attitude which is not limited to Hoffa and top officials; it is echoed down through the ranks as well. A Teamsters member once told P. J. Siemiller, international vice-president of the Machinists, that "I don't care what Jimmie Hoffa does with my four dollars a month—he can shoot craps on the White House lawn if he wants to—so long as he keeps up the present conditions." [9] The scandals about Beck and Brewster caused only a mild ripple among the union's rank and file. "Everybody is out to get what he can," a Minneapolis driver observed. "Let the big boys fight it out on their own—I'm doing all right." [10] It is complacency, not fear, which prompts this attitude. And although it is dramatized among the Teamsters members, it is not uncommon within unions which boast of their democratic procedures and membership controls.

What has happened is that a gradual change has been taking place within the labor movement, a change which received its initial impetus, paradoxically, during the great organizing drive of the 'thirties. In place of the camaraderie of the closed shop, there has come the union shop with its emphasis on making the "free rider" pay his share of the organization's maintenance. Under the old craft unionism, a skilled worker would serve his apprenticeship under the guardianship of the union, proudly establish his claim to journeyman status through his union book, and remain a member of the union throughout his life. It was his second home, the source of his job, the defender of his craft. The worker's loyalty to the union outdistanced his loyalty to his employer, and his dog-eared union book was a guarantee of security and remained in his wallet through good years and bad.

This situation no longer holds true. The union's exclusive claim to the membership of the journeyman was destroyed by the Wagner Act, which established National Labor Relations Board elections as the measure for union representation. So today a worker may join a different union each time he shifts his job. And if he should get hired at an unorganized plant, although at the same job, he would not join a union at all. Union membership has become related to the offering of service rather than to a basic fraternity upon which unions were founded. In some areas the unions have contracted with employers for an "agency shop" clause, under which nonmembers need not join the union but merely pay the union an "agency fee," equivalent to normal dues, for the services they receive.

This is a still-developing phenomenon and does not apply universally. Among some unions, there remains an abiding belief in membership participation which results in constant efforts by the officialdom to rouse membership interest, increase rank-and-file participation, and justify the traditional democratic processes. But what we have seen in the Teamsters is not peculiar to one union, nor have the idealistic experiments in democratic participation (although occasionally successful under the guidance of inspired leadership) provoked widespread imitation. We are witnessing the development of an organization-membership relationship which can be seen in full flower among the cooperative mutual insurance societies, where the member relies upon the organization for the furnishing of specific services and has little interest in its leadership or internal operations. What we may see in the future is an "auto-club" unionism—for a fee, the organization will supply such services as collective bargaining, grievance handling, and protection on the job.

Unlike the insurance societies and auto clubs, however, unions do not function under the American system of collective bargaining except by total representation. The time is long past when a union was truly the voluntary association it still maintains as a legal fiction. If auto-club unionism becomes universal, it presents us with tremendous social implications. The law now allows workers to exercise a veto on union power in three ways—certification, decertification, and deauthorization. Under certification, workers may choose by majority vote whether to have the union represent them in bargaining, and if a union already holds bargaining rights, a rival may seek to replace it when the current contract expires. Decertification is the reverse of this process. It allows the workers to cancel the union's bargaining rights through an election, although here again the process cannot interfere with the contract. Decertification is a dangerous process from a worker's point of view because, if the union loses, he is left defenseless unless another union quickly steps into the vacuum. The third process, deauthorization, is directly related to the concept of auto-club unionism, although it is little known and rarely used. In a deauthorization election, the workers may vote to void the "union shop" contract clause which provides that workers must pay dues as a condition of employment, and thus forces a union leadership to make certain that its "service" obligations are fulfilled if the union is to continue to collect its fees.

The legal remedies of certification and decertification can be frustrated by an agreement among unions not to trespass on each other's bargaining jurisdictions—a "no raiding" pact is written into the AFL-CIO constitution. Such an agreement, given the establishment of auto-club unionism, would invite the same legal prohibition which now bars collusive monopolistic practices among corporations. Moreover, the abuses and malpractices which are inevitable under auto-club unionism would soon lead to government regulation of unions which would make the Landrum-Griffin bill a model of lenient intervention.

Whether auto-club unionism, a caricature of traditional unionism, comes to pass will depend not so much on the leadership as on the membership of unions. There have been few cases where leaders have been able to inspire an apathetic membership but the way is clear—in the Teamsters constitution as in the constitutions of other unions—for an aroused membership to make over the unions into truly democratic organizations. But there is much doubt that such is the shape of the future; to most members, as Hoffa said, running the union "is the business agent's job." And the business agent rarely disagrees.

Footnotes

CHAPTER ONE

1. *Select Committee on Improper Activities in the Labor or Management Field Hearings,* Part 40, Sept. 18, 1958, p. 15287 (hereinafter referred to as *Select Committee Hearings*).
2. *New York Times,* July 4, 1958.
3. *Second Interim Report of the Select Committee on Improper Activities in the Labor or Management Field,* Aug. 5, 1959, p. 110 (hereinafter referred to as *Second Interim Report*).
4. *International Teamster,* March 1961, p. 29; Feb. 1959, p. 37.
5. *International Teamster,* Jan. 1962, p. 6.
6. *Officers Report,* 1961 Convention, pp. 42–43; *International Teamster,* March 1961, p. 29, Dec. 1961, p. 29, April 1962, pp. 30–31.
7. *Secretary-Treasurer's Report,* 1957 Convention, p. 11; *Officers Report,* 1961 Convention, p. 42.
8. *Secretary-Treasurer's Report,* 1957 Convention, pp. 42–49; *Officers Report,* 1961 Convention, pp. 53–56.
9. *International Teamster,* Feb. 1959, p. 31.
10. *Ibid.*
11. *1961 Convention Proceedings,* First Day, pp. 71–130.
12. *Fortune,* May 1941, p. 97.
13. *Ibid.*
14. *1957 AFL-CIO Convention Proceedings,* Volume I, p. 70.
15. *Officers Report,* 1961 Convention, p. 17.
16. R. D. Leiter, *The Teamsters Union* (New York: Twayne Publishers, Inc., 1957), p. 17; Teamsters News Service, *The Teamsters Story,* Sept. 17, 1957.
17. *International Teamster,* Oct. 1920.
18. Leiter, *op. cit.,* pp. 22–26; *1952 Convention Proceedings,* p. 30.
19. Tobin used the growing power of the AFL to defeat the rival union, demanding that AFL central bodies oust the secessionists. See *1908 AFL Convention Proceedings,* p. 167.

20. *Constitution,* 1901, Sections 1, 2.
21. *Constitution,* 1908, Section 2.
22. *Constitution,* 1961, Article I, Section 2.
23. See membership tables, Leiter, *op. cit.,* pp. 33, 39.
24. *Constitution,* 1901, Section 4; *Constitution,* 1906, Section 4; *Constitution,* 1908, Section 3.
25. James A. Brownlow, president of the AFL-CIO Metal Trades Department; *1961 Metal Trades Department Convention Proceedings,* p. 6.
26. *1909 AFL Convention Proceedings,* p. 301; *1910,* pp. 287–289.
27. Status of Free Men, Minneapolis: Milk Drivers Local 471, 1947, pp. 7–9; *1925 Convention Proceedings,* p. 34; *International Teamster,* June 1938; J. B. Gillingham, *The Teamsters Union on the West Coast,* Berkeley: Univ. of California, 1956, pp. 54–59; S. E. Hill, *Teamsters and Transportation,* Washington: American Council on Public Affairs, 1942, pp. 95–97; *1937 AFL Convention Proceedings,* p. 483.
28. *1946 AFL Convention Proceedings,* p. 135; Gillingham, *op. cit.,* pp. 53–54; *Constitution,* 1947, Article II, Section 1; *Constitution,* 1952, Article II, Section 1; 1961 Teamsters *Constitution,* 1961, Article II, Section 1.
29. Gillingham, *op. cit.,* pp. 3–5; *Newsweek,* Dec. 15, 1958, p. 58; *International Teamster,* Sept. 1959, p. 2; Dec. 1959, p. 8; June 1960, p. 17; Jan. 1961, p. 11; *1961 Convention Proceedings,* Third Day, pp. 42–46.

CHAPTER TWO

1. *Constitution,* 1961, Article III, Section 1.
2. *Minneapolis Tribune,* July 3, 1961; *1961 Convention Proceedings,* First Day, p. 4; Third Day, pp. 18, 61; Fourth Day, p. 85; Fifth Day, p. 23.
3. *Constitution,* 1961, Article III, Section 2.
4. *International Teamster,* April 1961, p. 6; *Official List of Delegates,* 1961 Convention.
5. *Constitution,* 1961, Article III, Section 5; *1961 Convention Proceedings,* Third Day, pp. 90–106, 113–124.
6. *Select Committee Hearings,* Part 40, pp. 15124–15125; *New York Times,* Oct. 24, 1957, Sept. 25, 1957; *1957 Convention Proceedings,* pp. 60–62, 442–444; *International Teamster,* April 1961, pp. 7–8; *1961 Convention Proceedings,* Second Day, pp. 90–91.
7. *New York Times,* Aug. 15, 1947; *1961 Convention Proceedings,* Third Day, Night Session, p. 79.
8. *1961 Convention Proceedings,* Fifth Day, p. 42.
9. *Ibid.,* Fourth Day, pp. 180–181.
10. *Constitution,* 1961, Article III, Section 8.
11. *1952 Convention Proceedings,* p. 89; *1957 Convention Proceedings,* p. 99; *International Teamster,* July 1961, p. 3.
12. *1952 Convention Proceedings,* pp. 90–92; *1961 Convention Proceedings,* First Day, p. 131.
13. *1920 Convention Proceedings,* Fifth Day, p. 40.
14. *1940 Convention Proceedings,* Fifth Day, pp. 22–26.

15. *1952 Convention Proceedings,* pp. 185–187.
16. *Constitution,* 1961, Article III, Section 8.
17. *1952 Convention Proceedings,* pp. 104–108.
18. *1957 Convention Proceedings,* pp. 417 ff.
19. *1961 Convention Proceedings,* Fourth Day, pp. 52–56.
20. *1961 Convention Proceedings,* Fourth Day, p. 113. The stenographic reporter corrected Hoffa's grammar in the official record and made it "Hoffa doesn't have any machine."
21. *New York Times,* Oct. 1, 1957; *1957 Convention Proceedings,* pp. 311–324. The committee on officers reports at the 1957 convention, incidentally, performed the unusual feat of passing by the deterioration of AFL-CIO relations without a single comment, though Beck's printed report discussed the issue and both Beck and English discussed AFL-CIO policies at length in their oral supplements to the printed documents.
22. *1961 Convention Proceedings,* Third Day, Night Session, pp. 81–122; Fourth Day, pp. 146–147, 151–153, 190, 191–200.
23. *Constitution,* 1961, Article II, Section 4.
24. *Ibid.,* Article IV, Section 2.
25. *1952 Convention Proceedings,* pp. 283–286; *1957 Convention Proceedings,* pp. 557–588; *1961 Convention Proceedings,* Fifth Day, p. 41.
26. D. W. Salmon, *Summary of Election Results,* St. Louis, 1957.
27. *Minneapolis Tribune,* July 4, 1961; *International Teamster,* August 1961, pp. 37–40.

CHAPTER THREE

1. *Constitution,* 1961, Article VI, Section 1.
2. *Ibid.,* Article VI, Section 1.
3. *Ibid.,* Article VI, Section 2.
4. *Ibid.,* Article V.
5. *1957 Convention Proceedings,* p. 415.
6. U.S. Department of Labor, Bureau of Labor-Management Reports, Labor Organization Financial Report, File No. 000093, for the year ending Dec. 31, 1960, Schedule F.
7. *International Teamster,* May 1930, pp. 9–10.
8. Richard L. Neuberger, *Our Promised Land* (New York: Macmillan Co., 1939), p. 182; *New Republic,* Aug. 1, 1949, p. 16.
9. *New York Times,* June 27, 1953.
10. *New York Times,* Oct. 13, 1954; *Minneapolis Star,* Oct. 18, 1954.
11. *1957 Convention Proceedings,* p. 500.
12. The biographical material on Hoffa, including the quotations, is taken from *The Name Is Hoffa,* a laudatory sketch published in 1956 by the St. Louis joint council in connection with a testimonial dinner.
13. *1952 Convention Proceedings,* p. 291.
14. *New York Times,* Nov. 8, 1958.
15. See also *Select Committee Hearings,* Aug. 19, 1957, Part 12, pp. 4809–4868.

16. *New York Times,* March 23, 1956; March 25, 1956; March 27, 1956.
17. *Select Committee Hearings,* Nov. 4, 1957, Part 16, pp. 6427–6549.
18. *Second Interim Report,* Aug. 5, 1959, p. 203.
19. *Second Interim Report,* Aug. 5, 1959, p. 207.
20. *Second Interim Report,* Aug. 5, 1959, pp. 144, 151.
21. The subject is a controversial one and the reader seeking more enlightenment may find it helpful to read the committee findings and the company memorandum and staff reply, *Second Interim Report,* Aug. 5, 1959, pp. 120–207.
22. *Second Interim Report,* Aug. 5, 1959, pp. 174, 175.
23. The platform's text is taken from the *Midwest Labor World,* Aug. 1, 1957.
24. Summaries of the committee's findings are contained in Select Committee, *Interim Report,* March 24, 1958, pp. 162, 221, 222–254, 443–449; *Second Interim Report,* Aug. 5, 1959, pp. 1–112, 113–119, 120–207; *Final Report,* Part 3, March 28, 1960, pp. 570–731.
25. Paul Jacobs, "Hoffa and the Underworld," *Dissent,* Autumn 1959, p. 436.
26. *1961 Convention Proceedings,* Fifth Day, p. 43.
27. 1958 Central Conference of Teamsters, *Chairman's Report,* p. 3.
28. Select Committee, *Final Report,* Part 3, March 28, 1960, p. 725.
29. *International Teamster,* May 1960, p. 33.
30. George W. Taylor, "Public Responsibility of Unions in Collective Bargaining," in *Labor's Public Responsibility* (Madison, Wis.: National Institute of Labor Education, 1960), p. 20.
31. Select Committee, *Final Report,* Part 3, March 28, 1960, p. 725; *Select Committee Hearings,* Part 37, Aug. 15, 1958, p. 13942; Interview with author, May 21, 1959.
32. *Select Committee Hearings,* Part 56, July 14, 1959, p. 12821; *1961 Convention Proceedings,* First Day, p. 41.
33. The Board of Monitors is more fully explored in Sam Romer, "The Teamster Monitors and the Administration of the International Union," Industrial Relations Research Association, *1961 Spring Meeting Proceedings,* pp. 604–613.
34. *International Teamster,* Nov. 1958, p. 12; *New York Times Magazine,* March 26, 1961, p. 9; *International Teamster,* May 1960, p. 34; *Minneapolis Tribune,* March 18, 1958.
35. *1961 Convention Proceedings,* Third Day, pp. 20–25.
36. *New York Times Magazine,* March 26, 1961, p. 9; *1961 Convention Proceedings,* Fifth Day, pp. 51–52; *International Teamster,* May 1960, p. 34; *Ibid.,* Feb. 1959, p. 30.

CHAPTER FOUR

1. *1947 Convention Proceedings,* pp. 247–261.
2. Interview with Beck, July 8, 1959.
3. *1957 Convention Proceedings,* pp. 51–54.
4. *Midwest Labor World,* Oct. 1, 1958.

5. *1957 Convention Proceedings*, p. 47.
6. *Select Committee Hearings*, Part 27, April 18, 1958, pp. 10696–10702.
7. *Constitution*, 1961, Article VII, Section 7.
8. *Ibid.*, Article VII, Section 1.
9. *International Teamster*, Dec. 1961, p. 28.
10. *Ibid.*, Feb. 1959, p. 27.
11. *Initial Report of Board of Monitors*, Part II, Exhibit 29, July 22, 1958.
12. *Teamsters News Service*, July 8, 1960; *International Teamster*, May 1960, p. 20.
13. *Teamsters News Service*, July 8, 1960.
14. *Constitution*, 1961, Article VII, Section 3.
15. *Ibid.*, Article VII, Section 4.
16. *International Teamster*, March 1961, p. 29.
17. *1961 Convention Proceedings*, Third Day, Night Session, pp. 79–124.
18. *International Teamster*, Dec. 1961, p. 28.
19. *1930 Convention Proceedings*, Fifth Day, p. 43; *1929 AFL Convention Proceedings*, p. 18.
20. *1952 Convention Proceedings*, pp. 241–242.
21. *International Teamster*, July 1957, pp. 8–9.
22. 1961 Convention, *Officers Report*, pp. 32, 40; *International Teamster*, March 1961, p. 29.
23. *1957 Convention Proceedings*, pp. 44–45, 491–498.
24. *1961 Convention Proceedings*, Article XI.
25. *New York Times*, Jan. 14, 1960.
26. *Constitution*, 1961, Article IX.
27. *Ibid.*, Article IV, Section 1.
28. *Ibid.*, Article IV, Section 1.
29. *Minneapolis Tribune*, Oct. 30, 1956.
30. *International Teamster*, March 1958, p. 5; Hoffa to joint councils, March 30, 1958; Hoffa to local unions, April 1, 1958.
31. *Constitution*, 1961, Article VI, Section 8.
32. *Ibid.*, Article VIII, Section 7.
33. *Ibid.*, Article VIII, Section 1, 5.
34. *Ibid.*, Article VIII, Section 6.
35. Interview with Hoffa, July 7, 1959.

CHAPTER FIVE

1. *Select Committee Hearings*, Part 48, March 15, 1959, p. 17678.
2. *1961 Convention Proceedings*, Second Day, pp. 12–13.
3. *1930 Convention Proceedings*, Fifth Day, p. 55.
4. The payroll data are taken from the *Labor Organization Financial Report* for the year ending Dec. 31, 1960, filed with the U.S. Department of Labor, Bureau of Labor-Management Reports, Schedule F.
5. *International Teamster*, Dec. 1958, p. 7.
6. *Select Committee Hearings*, Part 49, Exhibit 49, p. 18095.
7. *Minneapolis Tribune*, Dec. 22, 1957; June 5, 1961.

8. *Select Committee Hearings,* Part 36, Aug. 8, 1958, p. 13585; *Minneapolis Tribune,* July 7, 1961.
9. *1961 Convention Proceedings,* Second Day, pp. 73–79.
10. *International Teamster,* Nov. 1959, p. 14; Jan. 1962, pp. 26–28.
11. *Miami Herald,* April 25, 1960; *1961 Convention Proceedings,* Second Day, p. 21; *International Teamster,* Jan. 1961, p. 2.
12. Interview with McCarthy, then director of public relations, July 21, 1959.
13. *Initial Report of the Board of Monitors,* Part I, Supplemental Report, May 27, 1958, p. 189.
14. *International Teamster,* Oct. 1959; May 1960.
15. *International Teamster,* June 1961, pp. 5–10; *New York Times,* March 17, 1961; *International Teamster,* Jan. 1962, pp. 20–22; *DRIVE Reporter,* June 1961, p. 8.
16. *International Teamster,* May 1959, p. 9.
17. *Teamsters News Service,* Aug. 7, 1960; *International Teamster,* Nov. 1959, p. 8.
18. Irving Bernstein, *The Politics of the West Coast Teamsters and Truckers,* University of California Institute of Industrial Relations, 1958, p. 19.
19. *1941 Western Conference of Teamsters Proceedings,* pp. 133–139.
20. *Teamsters News Service,* Oct. 30, 1959.
21. *Ibid.,* July 8, 1960.
22. *Teamsters News Service,* Aug. 7, 1959; March 4, 1960; *International Teamster,* March 1961, p. 29; Feb. 1959, p. 37; Associated Press dispatch from Washington, Oct. 23, 1960.
23. *International Teamster,* Oct. 1960, p. 11; *St. Paul Dispatch,* Oct. 4, 1961; *Teamsters News Service,* Aug. 19, 1960; *International Teamster,* Oct. 1960, p. 9; *Teamsters News Service,* Oct. 21, 1960; *Midwest Labor World,* Dec. 1960.
24. *International Teamster,* Dec. 1960, pp. 4–6.
25. *Minneapolis Tribune,* July 3, 1961; *1961 Convention Proceedings,* Third Day, pp. 31–32; *International Teamster,* Dec. 1961, p. 10.
26. *1961 Convention Proceedings,* Third Day, pp. 37–40.
27. 1961 Teamsters Convention, *Officers Report,* p. 45.

CHAPTER SIX

1. *Constitution,* 1961, Article XV, Section 7.
2. *The Name Is Hoffa,* Detroit, 1955, p. 12.
3. *1957 Convention Proceedings,* pp. 388–397.
4. *Northern California Teamster,* Aug. 23, 1961; *International Teamster,* Oct. 1961, p. 11.
5. 1961 Convention, *Officers Report,* p. 12.
6. *Western Conference of Teamsters Report,* Feb. 10, 1961.
7. Interview with Hoffa, Dec. 2, 1961.
8. Select Committee, *Second Interim Report,* Aug. 5, 1959, pp. 120–187.
9. *Minneapolis Tribune,* Aug. 6, 1961.
10. Select Committee, *Final Report,* Part 3, Mar. 28, 1960, pp. 636–644.

11. *International Teamster,* Oct. 1960, p. 15; New Republic, Oct. 3, 1960, p. 7.
12. *1957 Western Conference of Teamsters Proceedings,* p. 5.
13. 1961 Western Conference of Teamsters, *Officers Report; Southern California Teamster,* Oct. 18, 1961.
14. *International Teamster,* April 1962, pp. 8–11; 1961 Central Conference of Teamsters, *Chairman's Report.*
15. *International Teamster,* Aug. 1945, p. 15.
16. 1958 Eastern Conference of Teamsters, *Chairman's Report.*
17. Interview with Miller, July 8, 1959.
18. *Western Conference of Teamsters Report,* April 29, 1960.
19. *1953 Eastern Conference of Teamsters Proceedings,* unpaged.
20. Gillingham, *op. cit.,* p. 14.
21. *International Teamster,* Oct. 1961, pp. 14–15; *The Machinist,* Nov. 10, 1961; Nov. 23, 1961; *New York Times,* Feb. 21, 1961.
22. 1961 Convention, *Officers Report,* pp. 6–7, 20.
23. *International Teamster,* Dec. 1961, p. 2.
24. 1961 Convention, *Officers Report,* pp. 47–52.
25. *International Teamster,* Oct. 1958, p. 6; Nov. 1958, p. 14.

CHAPTER SEVEN

1. *Minneapolis Tribune,* Dec. 30, 1952.
2. *Constitution,* 1961, Article VII, Section 3.
3. 1957 Convention, *Secretary-Treasurer's Report,* pp. 42–48; 1961 Convention, *Officers Report,* pp. 53–57.
4. *Constitution,* 1961, Article II, Sections 1, 3.
5. *1961 Convention Proceedings,* Third Day, p. 78.
6. *New York Times,* Aug. 1, 1953; Dec. 11, 1957.
7. *Constitution,* 1961, Article XVIII.
8. Philip Taft, *Corruption and Racketeering in the Labor Movement* (Ithaca, N.Y.: New York State School of Industrial and Labor Relations, 1958), p. 1.
9. Select Committee, *Final Report,* Part 4, Mar. 31, 1960, pp. 868–870.
10. *The Reporter,* Oct. 12, 1961, p. 45.
11. Taft, *op. cit.,* p. 1.
12. *Teamsters News Service,* July 10, 1959.
13. *1961 Convention Proceedings,* Fourth Day, pp. 153–154.
14. *Constitution,* 1961, Article IX, Section 9.
15. *Ibid.,* Article XIV, Section 2.
16. *Ibid.,* Article XXI, Sections 1, 2.
17. *Ibid.,* Article XXI.
18. *International Teamster,* Jan. 1961, p. 8.
19. *Proposed Model Local Union Bylaws,* published by the union, 1961.
20. *Constitution,* 1961, Article II, Section 4.
21. *Ibid.,* Article X, Section 5.

22. Samuel Hill, *Teamsters and Transportation* (Washington: Public Affairs Press, 1942), p. 192.
23. *Initial Report of the Board of Monitors,* Part I, May 27, 1958, p. 7.
24. Select Committee, *Interim Report,* Mar. 24, 1958, p. 237.
25. *Constitution,* 1961, Article VI, Section 5.
26. *International Teamster,* Feb. 1961, p. 19.
27. *1961 Constitution,* Article X, Section 3.
28. Interview with Hoffa, Dec. 3, 1961.
29. *International Teamster,* Nov. 1961, p. 8.
30. *Constitution,* 1961, Article X, Section 2.
31. *1961 Convention Proceedings,* Second Day, pp. 82–84.
32. *Constitution,* 1961, Article X, Sections 7, 9, 10.
33. *Ibid.,* Article XIII, Sections 4, 7.
34. *1961 Convention Proceedings,* Third Day, Night Session, p. 104.
35. *Constitution,* 1961, Article XIII, Sections 1, 12.
36. *Ibid.,* Article XII, Section 11.
37. *Ibid.,* Article XVIII, Section 1.
38. *Ibid.,* Article XVIII, Sections 6, 7, 8.
39. *Ibid.,* Article XVIII, Section 9.
40. *Ibid.,* Article XVIII, Section 2.
41. *Ibid.,* Article XVIII, Section 3.
42. *Ibid.,* Article XVIII, Sections 4, 10.
43. *Ibid.,* Article IX, Section 11, Article XVI, Section 1.
44. *International Teamster,* Nov. 1958, p. 7.
45. *Constitution,* 1961, Article XIX.
46. *The Brewery Worker,* Sept. 1960, p. 10.

CHAPTER EIGHT

1. *1899 AFL Convention Proceedings,* p. 29.
2. *1903 AFL Convention Proceedings,* p. 76.
3. *1933 AFL Convention Proceedings,* p. 394.
4. *1912 AFL Convention Proceedings;* Marc Karson, *Labor Unions and Politics* (Carbondale, Ill.: Southern Illinois University Press, 1958), p. 130.
5. *1917 AFL Convention Proceedings,* p. 423; *1930 Teamsters Convention Proceedings,* Third Day, p. 20.
6. Philip Taft, *The AFL from the Death of Gompers* (New York: Harper and Bros., 1959), p. 26.
7. A. H. Raskin, *New York Times Magazine,* Oct. 20, 1957, p. 19; *1957 Convention Proceedings,* p. 38.
8. *1934 AFL Convention Proceedings,* p. 453.
9. *1934 AFL Convention Proceedings,* p. 453.
10. Taft, *op. cit.,* pp. 107, 162.
11. *1930 Convention Proceedings,* Third Day, p. 25.
12. *International Teamster,* Jan. 1937, inside front cover.

13. *1952 Convention Proceedings*, p. 300.
14. *International Teamster*, May 1938, p. 14.
15. *Fortune*, May 1941, pp. 139–141.
16. *New Republic*, Aug. 1, 1949, p. 17.
17. Select Committee, *Final Report*, Feb. 26, 1960, Part I, p. 69.
18. *International Teamster*, Jan. 1959, p. 3.
19. *Labor's Daily*, Bettendorf, Iowa, Aug. 23, 1957.
20. *New York Times*, Dec. 3, 1959.
21. Leiter, *op. cit.*, pp. 86–92.
22. *1922 AFL Convention Proceedings*, p. 400.
23. Leiter, *op. cit.*, pp. 94–96; *American Labor Year Book* (New York: Rand School of Social Science, 1926), p. 111.
24. Leiter, *op. cit.*, pp. 94–100, 102–103.
25. *International Teamster*, Aug. 1943, p. 27.
26. Leiter, *op. cit.*, pp. 92–94; Gillingham, *op. cit.*, pp. 69–775; *International Teamster*, Aug. 1961, p. 19.
27. *New York Times*, Feb. 21, 1956.
28. *1957 AFL-CIO Convention Proceedings*, Volume II, p. 488.
29. *Ibid.*, Volume II, pp. 502–505.
30. *Ibid.*, pp. 311–323.
31. *International Teamster*, Feb. 1962, p. 12.
32. *1957 AFL-CIO Convention Proceedings*, Volume I, pp. 96–105.
33. *1957 Teamsters Convention Proceedings*, p. 625.
34. *Minneapolis Tribune*, Feb. 9, 1958.
35. *New York Times*, May 27, 1958.
36. *New York Times*, July 16, 1958.
37. *New York Times*, Aug. 19, 1958.
38. *International Teamster*, Nov. 1958, p. 6; *Midwest Labor World*, Sept. 15, 1958.
39. *1958 Chairman's Annual Report*, Central Conference of Teamsters, p. 4.
40. United Press International dispatch from Pittsburgh, Nov. 4, 1958; *International Teamster*, Dec. 1959, p. 5.
41. *International Teamster*, Nov. 1958, p. 14; *Detroit News*, Nov. 1, 1958; *Midwest Labor World*, Dec. 15, 1958.
42. *New York Times*, June 14, 1959.
43. *International Teamster*, Dec. 1958, p. 7.
44. *Teamsters News Service*, Sept. 18, 1959.
45. *1959 AFL-CIO Convention Proceedings*, Volume I, pp. 466–469.
46. *Ibid.* Volume I, pp. 309–311.
47. *Constitution*, 1961, Article IX, Section 12.
48. *New York Times*, July 7, 1961.
49. *1961 Oil, Chemical, and Atomic Workers Convention Proceedings*, pp. 49–50.
50. *New York Times*, Oct. 11, 1961.
51. *1961 AFL-CIO Convention Proceedings*, Third Day, pp. 29–40.
52. *International Teamster*, Jan. 1962, pp. 16–18.
53. *Chicago Tribune*, Dec. 13, 1961.
54. *International Teamster*, Jan. 1962, pp. 11, 16.

55. *1961 Convention Proceedings,* First Day, p. 10.
56. *1957 AFL-CIO Convention Proceedings,* Volume II, pp. 423–448.
57. *New York Times,* Jan. 25, 26, 27, 1962.
58. *Business Week,* July 19, 1958, p. 70; *International Teamster,* Aug. 1958, p. 13.
59. Release, International Transport Workers Federation, Nov. 5, 1958; *Select Committee Hearings,* July 14, 1959, Part 56, p. 19745.
60. *International Teamster,* Nov. 1957, p. 16; May 1958, p. 9.
61. *Railway Clerk,* April 1, 1960, p. 7; Western Conference of Teamsters, *Report,* May 13, 1960.
62. *1961 AFL-CIO Convention Proceedings,* Third Day, p. 37; *Teamsters News Service,* Feb. 9, 1962.
63. Western Conference of Teamsters, *Report,* Feb. 9, 1962.
64. Interview with Hoffa, May 21, 1959; *Select Committee Hearings,* July 14, 1959, Part 56, p. 19735.
65. *Ibid.,* pp. 19735–19736.
66. *International Teamster,* July 1960, p. 23.
67. *1961 Convention Proceedings,* First Day, pp. 6, 8.
68. *The Worker,* July 30, Oct. 8, Oct. 15, 1961.
69. *Business Week,* Aug. 13, 1960, p. 72; Feb. 3, 1962, p. 41.

CHAPTER NINE

1. *International Teamster,* Jan. 1934, p. 8.
2. Quoted in Richard L. Neuberger, "Labor's Overlords," *American Magazine,* March 1938, p. 167.
3. *Select Committee Hearings,* Part 3, March 14, 1957, pp. 1018–1019.
4. Edward Linn, *Saga Magazine,* March 1959, p. 77.
5. *International Teamster,* Nov. 1957, p. 44.
6. 1958 Central Conference of Teamsters, *Chairman's Report,* p. 4.
7. *Ibid.,* p. 4.
8. *Select Committee Hearings,* Part 40, Sept. 18, 1958, p. 15250.
9. Industrial Relations Research Association, *December Meeting Proceedings,* 1958.
10. *Minneapolis Tribune,* March 28, 1957.

Index